MIRACLE OF MIRACLES

*A Muslim woman's conversion to Christ
and flight from the perils of Islam*

D0111501

MINA NEVISA

WITH JIM CROFT

FOR ORDERING INFORMATION OR TO CONTACT THE AUTHOR:
MIRACLE OF MIRACLES by Mina Nevisa
Touch of Christ Ministries
P.O. Box 2861
Fairfax, VA 22031
e-mail: minanevisa@aol.com
Web site: www.touchofchrist.net

Unless otherwise noted, all Scripture quotations are from the New King James Version of the Bible (NKJV), © 1979, 1982, 1990, Thomas Nelson Inc., Publishers.

Copyright © 2004 by Mina Nevisa

All rights reserved

Library of Congress Control Number: 2004105507

International Standard Book Number: 1-883928-46-X

Printed in the United States of America

Second Edition 2005

05 06 07 — 6 5 4 3 2

DEDICATION

I am dedicating this book to the United States of America. The Lord has blessed you with glorious abundance in all things. The kindness and humility that are demonstrated through the generosity of your citizens is unique. Therefore, you deserve to know the truth about the tragic oppressions from which your graciousness has offered safe haven for so many. It is my prayer that God's blessings and His hand of protection will continually enable you to remain as His Miracle of Miracles in the global community.

Acknowledgments

I would like to express my warmest appreciation to my writing partner and editor, Pastor Jim Croft. His literary skills and vast knowledge of Islamic issues and Christian doctrines have proved invaluable. I would also like to thank everyone who tirelessly assisted me in the preparation of this manuscript and all who so graciously helped finance its publication. I bless each of you from the bottom of my heart.

TABLE OF CONTENTS

PREFACE

The book that you have in your hand was prayerfully penned with several goals in mind. First, it is the biography of the miraculous transformation of the life of Mina Nevisa, as related to Jim Croft. She was born into a prestigious family of fundamentalist Muslims in Iran. It relates the glories of her redemption through Christ and the price tag it carried for her as one reared in a radical Islamic society. Salvation is free, but its consequences can be costly. For her it cost family, exile from her homeland and the torture and martyrdom of her most treasured relatives and friends. You will be thrilled by the extraordinary things that God has done for her and through her and her husband's ministry. Most likely you will be shocked to learn the extent to which satanically inspired people will go to stop those who proclaim the message of the Cross. Kidnapping and death threats followed her and her husband to the shores of Christian nations. The vessels that did so had every confidence that they were performing a great service for Allah.

Secondly, hopefully it will be used by the Holy Spirit to alert Christians living in free democracies about the plight of this planet's billion plus Muslims. These poor souls have every aspect of their lives complicated by the doctrines of Muhammad. It is a needed wake-up call. It might provoke you to praise God that you do not live where there is the potential to awaken any morning to the news that your pastor has been executed for preaching the Gospel. Our prayer is that it might bring you to voice endless intercessions for the salvation of those who are living under the blackest of spiritual clouds, Islam.

Finally, the stories that you are about to read have blessed the thousands who have heard and read them. However, the inspiration that we anticipate for you will be incomplete if we fail to educate you about the true nature of Islam. To this end we have included an addendum titled, *Insights into the deceptions of Islam*. It will lead you on a trek beyond the liberal news media's politically correct assertions. Islam is nothing akin to a religion that promotes international peace and harmonious respect for those of other faiths. You will discover realities about the life of Muhammad and the societal woes that his teachings have produced in the nations that adhere to them. It challenges Muslim readers to objectively examine the tragic fruit that Islam has spawned. We are praying that all will become bold and enlightened witnesses for Christ through reading this book.

—MINA NEVISA AND JIM CROFT

Chapter 1

WEALTH, PRIVILEGE AND DISAPPOINTMENT

CHILDHOOD MEMORIES

It was a rainy fall October day in Tehran. Raindrops spattered against the full-sized window that spanned our living room. From the couch I could see our spacious yard's beautiful garden with its tall weeping willow trees and a portion of the street that passed in front of our home. At that moment, a sight caught my eye that symbolized something about my life that I would not understand until years later. It was a bee that was trapped behind the window that was banging itself against the windowpane as it struggled for freedom. I was to discover that, like that bee, though I was surrounded by beauty, I nonetheless was also a prisoner in the home of devout Muslims.

I am the youngest of seven children born to a wealthy fundamentalist Muslim family that resided in Tehran, the capitol of Iran, ancient Persia. It is located in the North West sector of Iran. Tehran's population is 16 million and Iran ranks as the 16th largest country on the planet. Iran's definition is "the land of the Arians." It is known for its marvelous *Elburz* mountain range, its gold and silver mines, vast oil and mineral resources, Persian rugs, artistic treasures, and its caviar. We Iranians are famous for our cordial hospitality.

I have two sisters and four brothers. The home of my parents was always a bustling center for family activities. I can hardly remember occasions when there were not multiple members of my older siblings' families visiting us. Our family home was a marvelously beautiful seven-bedroom estate of traditional Iranian architectural design. My father had spared no expense in its construction. Its opulent features fascinated all who visited us. Its windows were plentiful and large. The big front door gave entrance into a foyer that had a crystal candelabrum hanging from the ceiling that had 25,000 sparkling pieces in its branches.

Our home was located close to my school. As a sixteen-year-old girl, I was often filled with pride as my high-school colleagues who walked me home gazed in wonder that anyone could live in such a house. My mother also took great pride in our home. Neither of my parents would tolerate messiness. She was a meticulous homemaker who had a tasteful eye for designing home decors. People marveled at her skills. One summer she planted flowers in front of the windows with colors that specifically matched the draperies and Persian rugs of the house. When she shopped for furnishings, only the best would suffice. Undoubtedly, she was very grateful that she was married to a wealthy businessman and money for the home was never an issue.

Perhaps my favorite places were the garden and our living room. My family delighted in taking the tea that my mother made for us on the *samovar* each evening while sitting in the garden or in the living room. To make a good tea is an admirable art form among Iranians. Good teas are graded by quality of color, aroma and exquisite taste. My father usually bought fresh, delicious pastries for these occasions. When the box was opened, either our living room or the breezes of the garden would be filled with their luscious scents. It was my father's habit to drink at least two cups of tea, one after the other.

Long-stemmed roses always filled the large crystal vase that sat in the middle of the living room. Their pleasant fragrance permeated the atmosphere. Half of one wall was covered with framed pictures and the other portion with well-cleaned windows. In one corner there was an antique bookcase that housed some ancient handwritten books. Other shelves kept the books and manuscripts authored by my grandfather. Above all, it was the home of the most important item in my father's library, his highly expensive sixty-five-year-old Koran.

Next to the bookcase there were two other significant pieces of furniture. There was an armchair that was reserved especially for my father and a small handcrafted wooden table was placed beside it. The armchair was his refuge of relaxation when he returned from work each day. No one else dared sit in it. The table was the revered pedestal for the Koran that he read daily. My mother never allowed anything else on that table. His Koran was cumbersome to hold, as it was heavy and had ornate artwork crafted into its covers. My secret wish was to experience the feeling of sitting in his chair while reading that big Koran. At my insistence, my father promised to buy me a Koran someday that was even more costly and ornate than his own.

My father was a tall, big-boned man with gray hair. He was sweet and kind, yet a very serious man who seldom joked. When he did joke, the jokes were funny and made everyone laugh. He took his responsibility of providing for the family seriously and his giving spirit prompted him to frequently bless us with extravagant gifts. Until I confessed Jesus as my Savior, it was my conviction that he was the most loving father that anyone could have.

Though he had a gentle demeanor, there is no escaping the fact that he was also a fanatical, fundamentalist Muslim. Islam was the priority of my father's life. In addition to his mandatory Islamic prayers, he spent a minimum of two hours a day reading the Koran. He kissed it on each occasion that he picked it up or returned it to its sacred pedestal. He frequently mentioned that no matter how many times one reads the Koran, there will still be things that mystify one's understanding. Yet, it was his conviction that it contained useful teachings that could be found each time he repeatedly read it. Everything he said and did had to be in accordance with the strictest interpretations of Islamic law. His primary goal for himself and his family was that we be pleasing to Allah. We were important, but secondary in his considerations as he labored to achieve his goal.

My mother was an attractive green-eyed blond who did not look Iranian. Her attitude was exactly the opposite of my father's. Her priorities revolved around all that pertained to the comfort and welfare of her family. For her, religion was, at best, secondary. She was the daughter of a colonel in the Iranian army, which might explain her manner of organized discipline that ruled every aspect of life in our home. She constantly busied herself by attending to the needs of the household. Though she had servants to help with household duties, she reserved the cooking responsibilities for herself. She was surely one of Iran's finest cooks and everyone relished an opportunity to sit at her table. She frequently said that her wish was that her children would always be like an unbroken chain, flowing in unity with one another. For many years that wish was fulfilled. There was hardly a day that passed when there were not multiple members of my brothers' and sisters' families present at mealtimes in our home. My brothers-in-law often complimented mother by saying that her cooking was superior to that of their own mothers.

In relation to my mother's attitude toward religion, it could be that her enthusiasm was dampened by the demands that Islam put upon her. Her father died when I was two. According to Islamic law, when a parent dies, the oldest child has the obligation to daily say the *Namaz* for them. *Namaz* is the Iranian word for the Arabic term *Salat.* The *Salat* is a ritual of daily prayers that are to be repeated 17 times each day. On behalf of her father she offered two units at dawn, four in the early afternoon, four in the late afternoon, four after sunset and three units after dark. In other words, in addition to all of her other duties, she felt compelled by Islam to compensate for her father's missed opportunities for prayers and fasts that supposedly pleased Allah.

FAMILY ACCOMPLISHMENTS

From my early years I was very proud of my family's wealth and accomplishments. Most of my male relatives were mullahs and many held various prestigious positions within the religious government of our nation. My parents insisted that all Muslims should be well educated and attain fluency in at least one foreign language. My six brothers and sisters were all graduated from the University of Tehran. Each studied different majors and became fluent in Arabic, English or French. With the exception of my youngest brother, who was a student of Arabic literature, all of my siblings were married by the time I left Iran. My youngest brother later became an engineer.

My two elder brothers, Morteza and Mohammad, were involved with my father's business, and the third brother was in the Persian-rug business. His name was Mehdi and he eventually became an eye doctor. Mandana, my oldest sister, was fluent in English and became a heart surgeon. Several European magazines that featured articles regarding successful Muslim women interviewed her. She married the brother of a famous judge of Tehran. Her husband was a mullah and a professor of philosophy in the University of Tehran. He was a polite and very responsible husband. My other sister, Mona, taught in the university and married a merchant whose father was one of the most successful millionaires in Iran. Interestingly, both of my brothers-in-law, unlike many Muslim husbands, permitted their wives to work even though money was not an issue in their households.

My father was a uniquely industrious man. At the age of nine, he and a childhood friend vowed that one day they would go into business together. They became partners in a successful leather factory that employed more than a hundred people. In addition he earned a masters degree in Arabic literature. He spoke and read Arabic with such fluency that he served as a Persian-Arabic interpreter. In keeping with his motto that hard work is a part of a Muslim's life, he also became a professor of Islamic theology at the University of Tehran. The trust and reliability that he had in his business partner freed him to give himself to his university work and his studies. His chief joy was teaching. He always said, "Joy, sorrow, wife, children and all of life are to be treasured as long as they do not trespass Islam and adherence to the *Sharia*" (the rules and laws of Islam).

BELOVED GRANDFATHER

One of the many things that gave me security in the years of my youth was my confidence that I was the favorite grandchild of my father's father. In his later years, after the death of my grandmother who passed away when I was two years old, he moved in with my family. He was never a burden to us as our home was spacious and we all loved him dearly. In Eastern countries like Iran, and in most Arabic societies, a high value is placed upon the unity of the family and honoring senior citizens. Children are taught that it would be unthinkable to allow their parents to be confined to nursing homes. Even in the most difficult situations they are routinely invited to live with their children.

I loved to sit in my grandfather's lap as he told the story of how he and my grandmother had met. His unfailing love for his wife, years after her death, made a great impression on me.

Whenever he spoke of her he seldom failed to respectfully honor her memory by stating that she was the most beautiful and righteous woman that he had ever known. Though he was my senior by 55 years, I could comfortably confide most anything to him. He enjoyed the same status with many of my relative's children. One of his joys was the fact that I could not pass him without offering the sweetest face on earth an affectionate kiss.

Another of his delights was sweet food. As he advanced in age, though he in general enjoyed good health, it was discovered that sweets were not good for him. Against my mother's wishes, it was my joy to sneak sweets to his bedroom. She often caught me in the act and lovingly scolded me quietly, as to not have him overhear. She would laugh and shake her head assuring me that she loved him as much as everyone. She simply wanted us to cooperate with her efforts to protect his health. To his credit I must add, he always insisted that traditional Iranian kebabs and stews were best for one's health. He never transgressed Islam's rules by eating forbidden foods like pork. His instructions were that everyone should avoid western fast foods.

He was very wealthy and one of Iran's most respected authorities on Islamic issues. He was a fundamentalist Islamic high priest who was also a gifted and famous author. His wrote books about Islamic topics, the Koran, Islamic laws, analysis of the Koran and so on. Many were sold in the bookstores. At the time of his death he had authored more than 65 books. On occasions when I saw people reading one of his books I would proudly inform them that he was my grandfather. It was not unusual for them to respond by asking me to have him autograph their copy or to secure a signed photo of him for them. When I left Iran at age seventeen, his books and teaching cassettes remained in great demand.

He earned his living through his public notary business and by teaching the Koran and Islamic theology at the *Feizieh* Islamic center. His fame and business success enabled him to own a large estate in Tehran and to frequently travel to various nations. My grandfather's notoriety as an author and lecturer made significant contributions to the fame of the *Feizieh* Islamic center. It is located in the holy city of *Ghom,* which is south of Tehran. Muslims from around the globe enroll there to study different aspects of Islam. During their school years they wear Islamic clothing. Dependent upon their respective majors, post graduation many go on to serve in different levels as mullahs and imams in the Islamic clergy, the society of Islamic priests. Mullahs are Islamic priests and Imams are a higher level of mullahs. Some continue their studies in different majors in the universities. Those earning masters degrees can obtain high positions in the government since they are already mullahs. Many of these also hold positions as doctors, engineers and politicians. The highly educated can also preach Islam internationally.

DEATH OF A PATRIARCH

As my grandfather advanced into his seventies, he began to develop some health problems. He had aches in his back and legs and an eye condition that required surgery. In spite of his failing eyesight he continued to write and accept speaking engagements that demanded travel. His remedy to overcome his pains for a good night's sleep was just to eat a little yogurt. He avoided the use of sleeping pills. His cure for headaches was a cup of tea mixed with lemon. Regardless of his dietary disciplines, age began to catch-up on him. He had to limit his speaking engagements and traveled less frequently. Though it was his boast that he had never taken pills, he began to need prescribed medications.

In retrospect, I now recognize that he likely was aware that the time of his demise was drawing near. Every Muslim is obligated to make at least one pilgrimage to Mecca, Saudi Arabia. Grandfather had made six pilgrimages to *Mecca* during his lifetime. He asked my father to accompany him on a trip to *Meshhad*, one of Iran's holy cities. It is the site of the shrine of *Reza* who was one of the Islamic prophets. People went there to offer special prayers. The house felt curiously empty during that trip and it proved to be his last to offer such prayers. Upon his return, he began to get his affairs in order. He visited all of the people that he valued and made sure that all of his financial debts were settled.

One night during the month of *Ramadan*, around midnight, he commented that he was not feeling well. It is mandatory that all Muslims fast during the day and only eat at night during that sacred month. My parents attempted to discourage him from fasting because of his medical problems. Nonetheless, he would wake up in the middle of the night to eat, so he could fast all day. In the daylight hours he passed the time performing Islamic ritualistic prayers and reading his Koran.

That cold winter night was differently blacker than other nights. In fact, I think that winter was different from other winters and even that *Ramadan* was different from all others.

He spent at least two hours talking with my father in what appeared to be a solemn discussion. Before retiring he mentioned that for the first time in his life he could not remember whether or not he had performed his customary prayers. This concerned me. I began to wonder why he had been so anxious to see everyone and to settle his financial affairs. A little past midnight, I was in a deep sleep. I was awakened by the sound of my father's voice as he spoke in a distressed manner with my uncle. They were in the process of rushing grandfather off to the hospital.

I jumped out of bed. My grandfather saw that I was awake and standing at the door. Bravely I tried to think positively, but negative thoughts clouded my young mind. He looked at me kindly, and tenderly kissed my forehead. He was unable to stand as he whispered, "I love you my little girl." My mother was weeping and I began to weep also. He seemed as calm and relaxed as always when he told me to go back to bed. For me, sleep was impossible. I wanted to accompany him to the hospital. I could not rest without telling him how much I loved him. I soon found myself standing in the dark street in my nightgown kissing his hand and repeatedly affirming my love for him. As my mother looked on from the front door of our home, we watched my father's car disappear from sight carrying our family's patriarch. We sat hugging one another as we wept. My tears and my mother's intermingled and soaked our faces, hair and arms. That very night at the hospital my dear grandfather passed into eternity. His death was a great loss to all who knew him. Their compassionate friend and wise counselor, was gone forever.

My father chose to not comply with my grandfather's request that he did not want an extravagant funeral. It was his desire that such funds be given to the poor. Dressed in black and with visible sorrow, all of his family, friends, students and professional colleagues came to Tehran's national cemetery. The Muslim custom is to bury the departed in a white robe rather than placing them in a casket. It was a sorrowful event for all as the wise counselor with the beautiful smile was entombed. Our family was numbed. Though the seasons have drifted into years, his absence is continually felt. Today, with smiles and tearful eyes we reminisce about his kindness, stories and jokes.

Though it has been over two decades, I still have vivid memories of that fatal night. To this moment, the thought of it brings tears to my eyes. Like all who loved him, I miss him deeply. Unlike most others, my tears reflect the reality that he did not know Jesus and that I might not see him in heaven. My doubts about the potential eternal state of such a warm-hearted, humble and kind man are heartrending.

MY ISLAMIC INDOCTRINATION

I learned to say the names of the famous imams and prophets of Islam before I could correctly pronounce my parent's given names. The first words that I could write legibly were Allah and Muhammad. The reverential sounds of the Koran being recited and referred to were a consistent melody in our home from the earliest days of my remembrance. At age five, long before I could properly pronounce or know the meaning of its Arabic words, I memorized my first verses from the Koran. This was a great source of pride for my father that held rewards for me. Whenever I recited a verse without making a mistake I would get a hug of approval. Then he would say, "Go put on your shoes. We're going to the market and you can pick out whatever you like." On one such occasion, I told him that I wanted a world globe to put into my room. Upon our arrival home, I rushed to my room to place it in a special place. Over the years as I studied that globe, I found myself wishing that I might someday travel to the exciting countries that were named on it. I resided in Tehran, but my heart longed for adventures in remote areas of the earth.

HIJAB

When I was five years old my parents encouraged me to

17

begin wearing the *hijab.* It is the head covering of *Shia* Muslim women. Unlike the full-body-length burkas of other Muslim sects, it is worn like a scarf, only covering one's head. The edges can be pulled over one's face, if there is a need to hide one's facial features. It is a sign that a woman is in compliance with Islam's demands that all women appear modest before God and any man other than their husbands. Married women can be subjected to divorce by their husbands if they refuse to wear it. In strict Muslims homes, respectful women will adorn themselves with it if a male who is not an immediate family member enters the house. In present-day Iran it is a crime for any woman, including non-Muslims, to appear in public without a hijab. Its absence is considered a form of apostasy and is punishable by flogging, imprisonment and even death. As a little girl it was hard for me to orchestrate adorning myself with it. I did like it though, because it made me feel like an adult. By the time that I was a teenager, I had become accustomed to it and gave it very little thought. Several months after my conversion to Christ I put it aside as for me it symbolized the old bondages of Islam.

SALAT

According to Islamic law, girls at the age of nine and boys at the age of twelve must learn to recite the *Salat* prayers in Arabic. It is essential for it to be prayed at the right time and in the right manner each day. Muslims of non-Arabic speaking nations, such as Iran, put a high value on the proper pronunciation of the Koran's Arabic words. It is their belief that doing so, along with knowing the meaning of these words, increases the likelihood that Allah will honor their prayers. My father put such a high priority on learning Arabic for spiritual purposes that he hired a tutor to come to our home for two hours each week. She taught in Tehran's Al-Zahra Islamic University. This gave me a tremendous advantage over most non-Arab Muslims in regard to reading and understanding what the Koran actually says. The Koran is written in an antiquated

formal style of Arabic that is undecipherable to most unedu-
cated Muslims.

I also had another tutor whose company I enjoyed. It was
my brother-in-law who was a mullah and therefore an expert in
Islamic Law. My sessions with him ensued whenever I went to
his office to help with his paperwork. I would ask him questions about Allah, heaven, the beginning of the world, death
and so forth. At times he would laugh and question how a
young girl like myself could come up with such penetrating
queries. To the best of his ability, he patiently never failed to
provide me with conscientious answers.

This brings me to a certain area of lack in my life. It was
there in spite of my family's wealth and love for me. In a certain
sense, I never had an opportunity to truly enjoy just being a
child.   I was the youngest and my constant companions were
adults. I bypassed the playing with dolls stage as I thought it
was too childish. My main goal seemed to be attempting to
please my parents and the other adults in my life.

RAMADAN AND MOHARRAM

There are two Islamic holy months that have special places
in my memories of my youth, *Moharram* and *Ramadan*.
Ramadan falls during the ninth month of the Islamic calendar.
It commemorates Muhammad's visit from the angel Gabriel
who brought him the revelation of the Koran. Supposedly this
took place at the Dome of the Rock in Israel. The Mosque of
Omar was built on that site in the city of Jerusalem. All faithful
Muslims are expected to abstain from eating and drinking from
sunrise to sunset during the days of *Ramadan*. Each night after
the call to evening prayer they are permitted to eat.
Conservative Muslims, like those of my family, only eat twice
during the night, once after sunset and once before sunrise.

No one is exempted from fasting and saying their *salat*
prayers. My mother would kneel next to the window and recite
it for her dead father and herself. Children are awakened in the
night to eat, so they will learn to fast during the day. The

sounds of *Ramadan* still linger in my ears; the rustle of prayer rugs unfolding and family members stooping to sit or kneel; my father reading his Koran aloud (It was not unusual for him to read the entire Koran during *Ramadan* and he expected the same of us); the radio broadcasts of special sermons and prayers by well-respected imams; announcements of the exact time of daily sunrises and sunsets; and the clatter of eating utensils in the night as my mother prepared food for the family. Personally, I tried my best to fast. I found in hard to awaken during the night to eat, but my hunger normally enabled me to succeed.

It must be said that not all Muslims fast during *Ramadan* or even bow toward Mecca, Saudi Arabia, five times each day in Islam's mandatory daily prayers. They don't trouble themselves to arise before daylight to get out their prayer rugs and kneel before Allah. Few of them have an inkling of what a parched throat feels like when one has been denied liquids when *Ramadan* falls during hot, dry periods. Their bodies have never ached with cold because they abstained from body warming foods when the temperatures fell below freezing. They don't have a clue about the fullness of what the Koran says and what Muhammad actually taught. It is these types who foolishly assert that Islam is an ideal religion, because they have never inconvenienced themselves to suffer the disciplines that it takes to be a true Muslim.

Moharram commemorates the martyrdom of Islam's imams who have given their lives for the cause. It is a special time of ceremonial observances for *Shia* Muslims and it falls within the first month of the Islamic calendar year. To demonstrate mourning, everyone wears black and many make *nazrs* or vows. It is a solemn oath made before Allah wherein a person pledges to perform certain duties during *Moharram* as a tribute to the departed heroes of Islam. For instance, one of my mother's vows was that she would cook delightful foods to share with anyone, rich or poor, who came to our door. I especially liked it when she would make *zereshk polo* (traditional Iranian saffron seasoned rice with roasted chicken). The quantities needed required that she hire three caterers to bring two ovens to our home to prepare the meal. As the luscious aromas of her food drifted through our neighborhood, friends and strangers were not bashful about coming to our garden to enjoy a meal. They knew that it would be delicious and they believed it carried extra bonuses. The legend was that any food made due to a vow had a special anointing from Allah to heal the sick and to ensure continuing health for the healthy. They all assumed that Allah was pleased when people shared one with another. She would have the servants put small portions of each delicacy on plates so everyone could freely sample everything. Some were so bold as to bring containers to carry food home. Of course, all of the members of our family would inevitably appear to relish the meal. None of us could resist the high quality of basmati rice that she used and her incredible recipe for chicken. After our guests left, my brothers' and sisters' families would stay behind to help clean up. Islam teaches that those who help another fulfill a vow in any capacity will be blessed. It was a joy to be together, all at the same time, and to talk into the late hours of the night.

DISAPPOINTMENTS QUICKENED BY THE SPIRIT

Regardless of the fact that I had a comfortable life, I began to experience a shift in my thinking at the age of fourteen. My parents enrolled me in a famous, high-society, private high school. In addition, they secured a tutor to teach me English. From that point on, I began to seek avenues to pursue my own interests. Satisfying my parents was no longer my primary goal.

At this juncture, I now realize that the Holy Spirit was quickening my soul to be dissatisfied with Islam. Questions began to come into my mind that often brought rebukes when I mentioned them to my male relatives, especially my father. Why is it that *salat* has to be said in Arabic? Doesn't Allah understand *Farsi* and other languages of the world? Why do prayers that are to be honored have to be said at specific times?

Does Allah have office hours wherein he is only available at certain times?

Caring parents, fine clothes and a privileged education were no longer enough for me. I loved God and I longed for a meaningful, two-way relationship with Him. I felt smothered in the dark confines of Islam. Complete obedience to the *Sharia*, reciting my *salat* and reading the Koran left me feeling empty. I enjoyed the family fellowship that came with *Ramadan* and *Moharram*, but the enjoyment was short lived. Afterward I still found myself in a place of spiritual hunger. All of my prayers, fasting, reciting of Koranic verses in flawless Arabic and helping others fulfill their vows were to no avail. It seemed to me that Allah had abandoned me, if He indeed knew that I existed. I inwardly knew that something wonderfully significant was missing from my life.

I was soon to discover that the chains of Islam were harsher than I had ever imagined. I was shocked into the reality of my plight and sufferings of all who seek freedom of religion in Muslim-controlled nations. I saw my beloved family members demonstrate unimaginable cruelty and fanaticism in the name of Allah. All of this was brought about by my introduction to a wonderful book, the Bible. It led me to confess the most majestic of names as the source of my salvation, the name of Jesus. His ending of my disappointments is bitter and sweet. As I pen these words my spirit cries out as I kneel before God in anguish for the Muslim world. "Lord intervene by Your power and send them messengers to give them the Truth. Deliver the lost masses of Islam from its cruel grip. Vanquish the dark shadow that prevents my father and my entire family from seeing Your glorious light. I know that one ray of Your light will free them from the prison of Islam wherein the jailer is none other than Allah."

Chapter 2

THE HARD ROAD TO LIBERTY

A FAMILY OF READERS

Every member of my family was an avid reader. Practically
from infancy, my mother gave us little books that we could pre-
tend to read. As the older children attained sufficient reading
levels they were held responsible to read aloud to the youngsters. There was nothing that I loved more than to have one of
my parents or a sibling read stories to me. I insisted that they
read the storybooks loudly so I wouldn't miss a word. Due to
my mother's wise strategy, as I grew older, and could read and
write, my hobby was reading books on every topic imaginable.
Science books, the Koran, books about Islamic law and any
other book that I could get my hands on was a new adventure
for me.

Because my family was comprised of fanatical Muslims, there
was a category of books that I was expressly forbidden to
explore. I was not to exhibit the remotest interest in Christianity
or Judaism. I was not even permitted to be familiar with their
ideologies and claims. I will never forget the cold winter day in
which I ventured into the prohibited territory. It marked the
beginning of the transformation of my entire life and everything
that I knew and loved.

THE INTERRUPTED PRAYER

I remember that day as though it happened yesterday. I was concentrating on performing my *salat*. It was my intention to do four units at noon and four in the afternoon. I switched on a cassette recording of the Koran and dutifully spread my prayer rug. For Muslims these small pieces of material are used to prevent ones feet, knees and forehead from touching un-hallowed ground while bowing in prayer. I began my prayers and suddenly became painfully aware that once again I was having a one-way communication with Allah. It was like clouds of sorrow were blanketing my heart. I wondered about the source of this sudden sense of hopelessness. Disappointment flooded into my mind and I stopped in the midst of my prayers. I initiated the questions of my heart to Allah. "If you are the almighty God, why does it seem so useless to tell you the secrets of my heart? Where is your power to give me personal answers? Why do I have to speak to you in Arabic? Don't you understand my mother tongue of Farsi?" In anguish I cried loudly, "Am I an Arab or an Iranian?"

It then dawned on me that I had done something that was forbidden unless one's life is at risk. I had stopped my prayers before they were completed. Islamic law dictates that if one commits this offense they are required to begin their *salat* all over again. This realization did nothing but intensify my agitated state of frustration. At that moment I chose to vent my anger rather than starting a fresh recitation of my prayers. "A one-way relationship with Allah! What a farce! I must discover another way that will give me a two-way relationship with a God who compassionately hears and answers my prayers. All I'm asking for is the freedom to speak to you in the language of my birth." This event sealed my heart with the conviction that I must discover another religion that would give me a living relationship with God. In my heart I knew that I could no longer venerate a dead prophet that was still in his grave. To me, the risk seemed minimal. Islam was giving me no assurance that I was moving forward in my spiritual quest and every indication that I would have no lasting peace if I remained where I was.

BOLD QUESTIONS

That evening my sister and her husband came to dinner at our home. He was a teacher of Islamic Law. Respecting his opinion, I asked him two bold questions, "Do you really believe that we as Muslims are blessed and can have the assurance that Allah has forgiven us?" His response was sarcastic laughter, "Any Muslim that would tell you that he knows the answer to those questions does not know much about Islam. None of us knows if we are truly forgiven and blessed by Allah. It is written that provided we are obedient to the *Sharia,* it is possible that Allah might have mercy upon us. All of us hope that we are forgiven and that we will be blessed, but none of us have assurance about it. We don't even know where we will wind up in the afterlife. Besides, none of us have the right to question Allah and his Law."

His insensitive answer led me to make a sinful departure from Islamic tradition. I decided that the Arabic *Shahada* confession of faith that my parents had whispered in my ears when I was one month old had been ineffectual. It is a verse from the Koran that authorizes an infant to be called a Muslim. They whisper these Arabic words into their baby's ear, *"Ashadu an alahail-lallah, ashadu anna Muhammadan rasulullah."* (I witness that there is no God but Allah, and Muhammad is the messenger of Allah.) I had come to the conclusion that all of my other rituals in Arabic were equally impotent. I loved Allah and desperately wanted to please him. I simply could no longer wink at my questions as though they were nonexistent. From that point on, I would persist in the rituals, but with a forbidden change. I would only use my native Persian language, Farsi.

This action made me the target of outrage from my father and jokes from the other members of my family who heard me praying. To father, I was committing a grievous sin. For the others, it was a laughable sin. My younger brother kidded and taunted me, "Why make such a big deal out of saying the *salat?*

Just do it in the manner they tell you and get it over with quickly." Father's angry complaints that I was sinning and their jokes did nothing to deter me.

Finally, father could no longer tolerate hearing my rebellious recitations of the sacred *salat* in Persian. He bolted into my room in a fit of red-faced rage, "Why do you insist on being so adventurous? Allah will never condone your praying in Farsi. How could you make a joke about such a serious point of our religion?" With a look that he interpreted as insolence, I looked at him and began to ask questions, "So, Allah does not accept such prayers just because they are not uttered in Arabic? Don't you think that it makes him appear a little narrow-minded? Why should I pray in a language that is difficult for me to understand? Allah must be a racist if he only accepts prayers in a single tongue. Where is his power that you always assured me that he has? It would seem that if he were all-powerful, he would be able to understand multiple languages."

Father drew close to me and pointed his finger in my face and began to shout, "Stop it, stop it! From where are you getting all of this nonsense? You are never to discuss this with me again. From this point forward you will pray in the manner that you have been taught and there will no more silly questions from you. I am an authority on Islam at one of the world's foremost Islamic universities and when sincere people want answers about proper protocol in Muslim practices, they come to me. It is ridiculous that my own daughter does not know what she is doing in these matters. You have no need to bother us again with your silliness."

He stomped out of the room and slammed the door with such force that the wall shook. I was left sitting in my room in a state of fearful shock. In my misery I wrestled with him mentally. "Sure, he is comfortable saying the *salat* in Arabic. He is an expert in the language and can fully appreciate what he is praying. But, what about the millions of Muslims that have no idea what they are praying? For them it is merely a meaningless, repetitious, lifetime ritual."

As time passed the lessons that I received from my Koran teacher further convinced me that Allah was withdrawing farther away from me. I was living in the reality that I was a twentieth century slave of a seventh century religion. I had been taught that slavery ended in the 18th century. Inwardly I knew that as a woman in the Muslim world, I was not much better off than an ancient slave. Like millions of my Muslim sisters, remaining in Islam meant continual disappointment in regard to liberty. I longed for the freedom that I was born to enjoy.

In search of truth

The winter passed and spring arrived. As I looked out my window and saw life in bloom all around me, I searched for a ray of hope that would transform my barren winter into spring. I wanted to embrace a faith that would graduate me from nonsense into meaningful experiences with the living God. I had always had an appreciation for God's natural creation. It was as though the sounds of rivers gurgling, birds singing, and the rustle of leaves in the wind were God's peaceful voice to me. It was my thought that I might discover the Creator in His creation.

I had to find a path to freedom. In my quest, I delved deeper into literature and poetry. Religion had lost its meaning and different philosophic approaches began to attract my attention. I found poetry to be my safe haven. The poets provided me with the comfort that there were people who understood the sorrows of life as well as its beauties. Perhaps the world-renowned Iranian poet Omar Khayam expressed it best, "A muezzin from the tower of darkness cries, fools, your reward is neither here nor there!" Humanity that has no understanding of the purposes of the successes and the tragedies of life has a limited capacity to know the value of life. This is the mystery that the ingenious poets and philosophers have struggled to unravel throughout the ages. I had come to learn that being is a continuation of going, but where was I to go and to whom?

TROUBLESOME BOOK BRINGS LIFE

On the first Thursday of each month my parents hosted a gathering in our home in commemoration of the martyrdom of imams in Karbela. In these sessions an authority on Islamic history tells the tragedies of famous Muslim prophetic figures who were martyred. He purposely rehearses the tragedies of their lives in a manner that incites many of his listeners into an emotional frenzy. It was as though the success of the guest speaker was evaluated on the basis of the intensity of the mournful wails and volumes of tears that he could incite from his audience. The meetings at our home were always a success. It was large enough to seat 40 to 50 men and women separately in accordance with Islam's custom. The house would be cleaned beyond perfection and my mother would prepare volumes of refreshments for the guests. Above all, my mother inevitably made a tremendous contribution to the pool of tears.

On a night of destiny, the priest that was to speak in our home was Ayatollah Nategh-Noori. He presently serves as an influential member of Iran's parliament. Due to several factors I wanted to avoid the meeting. I never had enjoyed or found them beneficial. I always dreaded seeing my mother's tear-swollen eyes after the monthly meetings. I was in the midst of my own tragedy and did not care to have dead heroes' sorrows added to my trauma. My need to study provided me with an excuse to be exempted from the affair to visit the university library.

My brother-in-law was in attendance at the meeting and he offered to give me a ride to the library. Within 30 minutes I was sitting in the library with my schoolbooks opened. While concentrating on my math studies I casually shifted my leg into a more comfortable position. I happened to look down and saw a book on the floor. I picked it up and discovered that it was titled *Injil Sharif.* It was the first copy of the Persian Bible that I had ever seen. Previously I had seen French and English versions, but had no idea that it existed in my own language. I surmised that it must be the holy book of Christians. Strangely, there was no mark identifying it as a library reference book. I concluded that a student must have left it behind and I attempted to turn it in to the librarian. Even more curious was the fact that she insisted that no one had reported it as lost and that I should take it with me to study at home. I thumbed through several pages and did not understand anything that I read. That night I could not study any further. Something or Someone was compelling me to get that book home. In compliance with the librarian's insistence I took it home thinking that it would be interesting reading material.

When I arrived at the house I was grateful to see that the guests had departed. I thought that the Bible would be a pleasant surprise for the members of my family. I was met with just the opposite. I never imagined that the possession of a holy book of another religion could invoke a fanatical assault on me as a person. Before my eyes and to the alarm of my emotions, I witnessed the male members of my family being transformed from loving people into hate-ridden radical Muslims.

My father was sitting in his favorite armchair, my mother by the living room's big window and my sister and her husband were engaged in a conversation with them. Upon my entrance, I excitedly greeted everyone and proudly showed the Bible that I had found. Without hesitation my father arose from his place and loudly accosted me. His face was flushed with anger. Simultaneously my brother-in-law took the book from my hand and read its title to the group with a surprised expression, "This is a Farsi version of the Christian Bible."

My father then began his tirade, "Where did you get that book?" I told them of my experience in the library. He responded angrily, "We respect that book but it is not ours." Then holding it in his right hand, he shook it in my face, "Allah has given you a holy book, the Koran. You do not need another one. Take it back where you got it immediately. I want to respect you, so don't make me have to take it back myself. It is your responsibility to get it out of my house. You are to return it and you are to never touch books like this again. Is that clear?"

I uttered a meek yes, but nothing was clear at that juncture. I was reeling from humiliated embarrassment over my father rebuking me in the presence of the rest of the family. He had never acted in this manner previously. My youngest brother piped in, "Father why are you so upset? What is wrong with a person simply getting information about what others believe?" Father again arose from his armchair and blurted forth, "I will never let any daughter of mine read a Bible. All that she could ever need is in the Koran." He then turned on my brother, "What information do you need that you cannot find in the Koran? Without waiting for his answer, he continued, "We do not need the other people's holy books to get insights about anything. The Koran is sufficient for everything that we need to know." He then plopped down in his armchair and sullenly glared at me. My brother-in-law added one final shot, "You must learn to immunize yourself from the temptation to explore materials that might negatively influence your Islamic faith."

I became upset with myself. As a seventeen-year-old girl, I simply did not have the maturity to anticipate the bizarre fanatical reaction that my otherwise tranquil family members would have to a Bible. In tears, I promised to return it to the librarian and sought refuge in my room. Before retiring for the night, my mother came to my room and reminded me of my promise to take the book back in the morning. Though I was shaking with fright, I quietly whispered, "Mother wouldn't you like to read the book?" Her response was to sweetly reiterate the things that my father had said.

LIGHT IN MY DARKNESS

My father's explosive tirade and my sister's husband's words fueled rather than discouraged my desire to read that book. I became curious about what it might contain that could be so disturbing. This brought me to rebel against the cautions of others, and I decided to read the Bible from cover to cover. This was the first rebellious act of my life against the wishes of my parents. It was quickly followed by my first lie. The next day when I arrived home from school Mother asked if I had returned the Bible to the library, and I assured her that I had. The truth was that earlier that morning I had been awakened out of deep sleep by her call to breakfast. When I opened my eyes I had good reason to be alarmed. In the wee hours of the morning I had fallen to sleep with a flashlight in my hand that I was using to read the prohibited book. There it lay, in clear view, right in the middle of my bedroom floor. It must have slipped from my hand when I fell asleep. In hurried panic, I hid the Bible under the mattress of my bed. All that day I had been plagued with the apprehension that someone might discover it.

My reading time was late at night when I had the assurance that everyone was asleep. I read it with my head under my bed sheets. I used a flashlight to illuminate its words. To turn on the room's reading light would put me at risk of being discovered. Determinedly, I read on though the heat was so sweltering under the covers that I could hardly breathe. When one hand tired of holding the flashlight, I would switch off to the other hand. Over the next two nights I completely read the New Testament while under the sheets. I skipped the genealogy sections, as I was interested in finding out about someone called, Jesus. As I read, I became increasingly aware that there was something or Someone gently nudging me to concentrate on Him.

THE KIND MIRACLE WORKER

As the days progressed, I occasionally risked reading during the day while my mother was busied with the household and before father returned from work. The person called Jesus enthralled me. The many points in which His character and lifestyle were so different than those of Muhammad fascinated me. Unlike Islam's prophet, He did not instigate wars to extend His influence, nor did He amass a harem of wives and concubines to gratify worldly lusts. The manner in which He protected and honored women was comforting to me, because it was so different from that which Muslim women commonly experience from spiritual leaders and their husbands. Most

Muslim wives would secretly admit that they are little more than the subservient housekeepers and sexual toys of their husbands. Muslim spiritual leaders enforce the laws of Islam that keep women in that position. Muhammad never performed a single miracle. During the days of Jesus' earthly ministry, there was not a day that passed wherein He failed to perform numerous miracles. Healing the sick, stilling storms, and miraculously feeding thousands was as easy as breathing for Jesus. His Heavenly Father provided His every need, so He never had to raid caravans to provide for His disciples. His Father inspired Him with kind words of wisdom, liberation, and forgiveness for all of those who were snared in various sins.

The Allah of Muhammad was vindictive, harsh and unforgiving. I found the concept that one could know that they were forgiven refreshingly attractive. Christ was famous for His loving kindness to everyone and Muhammad was infamous for his unloving cruelties to those who opposed him. For me, the prospect of learning more about God while reading a book written in Persian, rather than Arabic, was delightful.

Simultaneous to my study of the Bible, I was experiencing a tremendous inward struggle. Reading about Jesus and learning about Christianity was fascinating, but it did not immediately overcome my misgivings about forsaking my allegiance to Islam. My whole identity was integrated with the Muslim world and it was difficult to consider any path that would hurt my loving family. To depart from the religion of my birth, I would need to have my many questions answered and a definitive confirmation from God. As the battle raged within I lived a double life. Secretly a man named Jesus captivated me and publicly I had every appearance of being a 17-year-old girl that was loyal to Islam. Even when I was in the midst of my Muslim rituals I was inevitably haunted by the awareness that there was something missing from my life. Therefore, no matter how hard I tried, it was impossible to concentrate on my Islamic duties.

All of this continued into the period of my upcoming graduation from high school. To please my parents and for the sake of my own future, it was essential that I achieve excellent scores on my final exams. Nonetheless, distracting thoughts came into my mind. Some of my questions about God were being satisfied and others were being generated as I read and reread the Bible. It would really be helpful if I could find people who understood the Bible to help me with my questions. I reasoned that the fact that there was a Bible in the Persian language was an indication that there must be some true followers of Jesus living in Iran. I really needed to find at least one Christian who could enlighten me about passages such as Matthew 11:28 where Jesus Christ says: *"Come to Me, all you who labor and are heavy laden, and I will give you rest."* Were those who were laden those who recognized that they were under the burden of unsatisfying religions? Or was it simply referring to the generic burdens of life?

A SPIRITUAL DREAM

One memorable afternoon I went to my room to perform my *salat*. As I knelt toward Mecca, I began to cry out to Allah. "God, I'm not sure that you really hear my prayers, because to date I've had no indications that I've been successful in my attempts to cultivate a two-way relationship with You. Here I am again crying out to You. I don't know who I am any longer. I feel as though I've always been the prisoner of a religious system and laws that were not of my choosing. The paths that I have taken to please You and to know You better have physically, mentally and spiritually exhausted me. I cannot take another step in my own strength. I beseech You to give me a sign that You care about me." The Lord let me know that He heard that prayer by giving me a spiritual dream that night. Its vividness will be forever captured in my heart and mind.

I was wandering barefoot through a hot desert. I was at the point of perishing from thirst and had become hopelessly lost in my search for water. I could not discern whether it was night or day as I stumbled along in a mixture of a dark and light mist. Suddenly, my attention was arrested by the sound of a loud voice, "I am the way, the truth and the life. No one comes to the Father except through Me." I had no idea that those words were found in the Bible. The penetrating sound of that voice caused me to awaken and bolt from my bed. As I did so, I was repeating the dream's message. Instantaneously, I understood that I must find a follower of Christ with whom I could share my dream.

That evening, my mother informed me that my brother-in-law and members of his family were coming for a visit to our home. This was a welcomed thought, as I was very fond of his twenty-eight-year-old sister, Monir. She too came from an influential fundamentalist Muslim family of wealth and she often gave me valuable advice as I was blooming into womanhood. She was a medical student that was soon to be graduated and licensed as a doctor. She was known to have long, gorgeous hair that was disguised by the hijab that she wore. During the meal she had announced that she had finally cut her hair. After dinner, I wanted to get her out of the presence of men so I could investigate her new hairstyle. Upon entering my room, my thoughts of joy turned to dismay. I had inadvertently left the Bible on my bedside table subsequent to my afternoon reading. I shuddered with fright as I envisioned my whole life turning into a hell. I could see the angry response of my father and the disappointment of my mother should Monir choose to brandish the evidence of my sin and rebellion before them. At that moment, I was sure that life, as I had known it, would soon come to an end.

Never would I have imagined the ensuing conversation that would transpire between us. Monir rushed over to the table, grabbed the Bible and held it fondly to her heart. Her eyes glazed with tears, she looked at me with a look that signaled that she was shaken and that her mind was reeling with dozens of questions. She collapsed on my bed and inquired, "Mina, do you read this book?" Without hesitation I responded affirmatively as though I was being guided by an unknown power. I took a seat beside her on the bed. I heard myself relating the whole story of my dissatisfaction with Islam, how I had found the Bible, my family's harsh response, my lies and the fact that I indeed read it and sensed an element of comfort as I did do. I confidently told her of my dream and my desire to discover the full implications of its interpretation. She then told me the story of her covert faith in Christ. I felt a closer kinship with her than I had experienced with any other person in my life.

Her face glistened with a joyous, tearful smile, "My sister, for the past eight years, I too have been hiding my Bible. I am a Christian. I came to know Jesus as my Lord through nothing less than a miracle. I met Him through my contact with a pastor who lived in Meshhad. We were introduced while I was a student at the University of Meshhad, prior to my transfer to the University in Tehran. He was present in a meeting that other students had invited me to attend. They sang Christian hymns and gave their testimonies about how faith in Jesus had transformed their lives. That first meeting changed my life. I accepted Christ into my heart and subsequently discovered that I have the call of an evangelist. To avoid the rejection of my family and to avoid detection and death, I have continued to wear the hijab and pretended to be an ardent Muslim. It has afforded me the privilege of testifying and distributing Bibles for my Lord."

Her testimony was interrupted by my mother's call for us to come and join the family for ice cream. We heard mother's approach up the stairs and she instinctively mimicked my strategy for hiding the Bible. She tucked it under my mattress. But before going down, Monir stood by the stairs and held my hands tenderly in her own as I looked at her in anticipation of her next words, "Jesus will show Himself to you sooner or later. Do you know why? Hallelujah, its because He is alive!"

I took courage in Monir's marvelous example of strength. It was awesome to learn of her empowerment to live a fruitful Christian life, regardless of the fact that two of her brothers were Islamic priests and her parents were extremist Muslims. Shortly after our discussion she telephoned and invited me to attend one of the secret prayer meetings of her Christian friends. I gratefully accepted her invitation, as there were many questions that she and her friends might be able to answer for me. My primary hurdle was to come up with a creative excuse to get out of the house. My father was lecturing in another city, therefore my mother let me go and meet with Monir without a clear explanation about what our plans were for the evening. We traveled by bus to the northern part of Tehran. When we entered the apartment, I was introduced to and warmly greeted by a mixture of about fifteen men and women. Monir shocked me as she removed her hijab in the presence of men. I knew she was a Christian, but my assumption was that the Lord would require that she remain veiled. I opted to keep mine on, even though I was self-conscious that I might appear as an ardent Muslim.

The meeting opened by a middle-aged man named Ali offering a prayer in Jesus' name. Then he led the group in singing songs of worship. The concept of worship songs was unfamiliar to me. However, I thoroughly enjoyed the lyrics about God's mercy and the melodies of the songs. Most of all, I was greatly impressed by the freedom of the people as they clapped their hands and joyfully smiled toward heaven. Their faces reflected the unfeigned peace that I was seeking.

Ali opened his Bible and handed it to me, requesting my participation by reading Psalm 100:2 *"Serve the Lord with gladness; come before Him with joyful songs."* He then proceeded to give a short sermon on the topic of sin. It was the first time that I had heard that all men were sinners. I was not offended, because knowing that I was still a Muslim, they were all amazingly friendly toward me. Had they visited a Muslim mosque, they would not receive a reciprocal warm welcome. Ali gave me some books about the faith and his telephone number. He encouraged me to give him a call at any time of the day or night in the event that I had questions or needed to talk. The meeting closed with a prayer for me. On the way home, I began to question Monir about the group.

Subsequent to that meeting, Monir and I drew closer than we had been at any time previously. It was a wonderful asset to have her as a sounding board for my visions of my future life. I devoured the reading material that had been given to me and attended more meetings at every opportunity. These opportunities did not come as often as I would have liked, because strict Muslim parents, such as mine, were hesitant to allow their daughters to wander the streets during night hours.

NIGHT OF ETERNAL DESTINY

Several months after my first visit to the Christian gathering, Monir called with exciting news. Pastor Hossien Soodmand, a clergyman from Meshhad, was to be the special guest speaker at the Thursday night meeting. My heart pounded with great expectations about meeting him. I had only seen a few Catholic priests on television and have never personally encountered any priests other than those of Islam.

The apartment was packed to the extent that there was standing room only. Monir and I were fortunate enough to find seats on the couch. We joined the others in exuberant songs interspersed with episodes of fervent prayers.

At first glance I discerned that Pastor Soodmand was a man of deep conviction, faith and humility. Kindness radiated from his face and his eyes sparkled with tears as He spoke on and on about the love that Jesus has for us. The longer he spoke, the more aware I became that my body was being energized by a strange, pleasant warmth. Suddenly that warmth exploded into a fire within me. It felt as though something was burning in my innermost being. At that same moment, everything in the room shined with a glorious light. Its source was the face of the minister. I knew that I must respond to that which I was experiencing. I slid from the couch to the floor. The shout, "Jesus I love you!" was begging to flow from my heart, through my vocal chords and over my lips for all to hear. In all of my years of Islamic rituals, I had never experienced such a sense of God's manifest presence.

With Bible in hand, the pastor started to step toward me. My words gushed forth, "I want to give my heart to this Jesus. Hallelujah, hallelujah, I want to belong to Jesus Christ!"

He took my hands in his and asked me some questions and then led me through a confession of Jesus as my Savior and Lord. "Do you want to give your heart to Christ?"

I sobbed with convulsive joy, "Yes, Yes." I urgently wanted him to understand that I really wanted to accept Christ.

"Are you ready to renounce Islam and all of the Islamic heroes that it venerates?"

I shook my head in agreement and everyone in the room extended their hands toward me in prayer, "Yes, yes I do deny Islam and all of the men that it historically honors."

"Then repeat what I am about to say with a loud voice that everyone can hear. Lord, today I confess my sins and I want to repent of all of them in Your Name. You are the Savior of the world. This day I give my heart to you. I believe that You died on the cross for me and that God raised You from death on the third day. I renounce all false prophets and all other religions, because I choose You this day as my Savior and Lord. In Jesus' Name, amen." My body was shaking from the first prayer that I had ever uttered in public as an expression of my faith in Jesus.

Pastor Soodmand encouraged everyone by stating that he sensed the presence of the Lord. He assured us that the proper response to His glory was to offer the Lord songs and prayers of adoration. We all joyfully complied with an hour or more of worship. As the meeting drew to an end he asked Monir to close with a prayer. Her prayer was a combination of cries of thanksgiving and praise for my salvation from sin. I rushed over to the pastor and told him of the story of my journey from being the daughter of dedicated Muslims to the child of Father God. At various points during my testimony he raised his hands and thanked and worshipped the Lord. I was greatly blessed by his prophetic insights about my future. He explained that the Holy Spirit inspired all of my thirst for spiritual life beyond Islam and my finding the Bible. He added that I could anticipate God's hand of loving care to continually overshadow my life and that God had chosen me to be His witness to my family and many other Muslims that would come to know Jesus. As Ali, Monir and I stood talking to him, he laid his hand upon my shoulder and pronounced a blessing and some cautions. "Mina, every Muslim who comes to Christ, is a miracle. Jesus has released you from bondage to Islam's legalistic laws and its regulatory does and don'ts that have governed every aspect of your existence. Do not ever let anyone or anything rob you of the freedom that Jesus has given you this night. Never allow any doctrine to hinder your bold proclamations that your Savior is alive. You can be confident that the angels are rejoicing with dancing and praises to God for your salvation through Christ."

Everything about Pastor Soodmand made a lasting impression upon me. His passion for Christ, his loving demeanor and his prophetic insights about my future enabled me to understand that the Holy Spirit would draw me further into the intimacy with God that I had longed for.

On the way home Monir confided in me that Pastor Soodmand had served as her example of a true Christian for her entire Christian life. He was the source of the Bibles and tracts that she distributed throughout Iran. She said that it was her desire to emulate his passion to see Muslims repent and be converted to Christ. She, like myself, found his genuine love for others and his willingness to serve people, rather than to be served, admirable. His enthusiasm gave her the courage to put her own life at risk by distributing Christian literature. She went on her missions veiled as a Muslim woman. She wanted to spend her life keeping the heavenly hosts exulting with joy over the number of Muslims that would come to Jesus as a result of her efforts.

Few Christians who live in free democracies can relate to the perils that face Muslims who convert to Christianity in Islamic-controlled states. To avoid embarrassment and to demonstrate their allegiance to Allah, the parents of these heaven-bound believers often covertly murder them before the authorities have a chance to find out about their conversions. Governments imprison, torture and execute them for apostasy from Islam. In 1990, Pastor Soodmand was arrested and tortured by the Islamic authorities that rule Iran. After four weeks he was released on bail to return to his four children and his blind wife, Mahtab. Subsequently, he was arrested again and imprisoned for a month. On December the third of that year he was executed by hanging. In an effort to insult Christianity they purposely killed him during the Christmas month. His wife and children were not informed of his fate until after it took place. Every Christian that knew this wonderful man who was martyred for his faith in Christ mourns him to this day. At every remembrance of his sweet eyes, his kind face, and his gracious gift of encouragement, I cannot help overflowing with tears. He forever holds a special place in my heart, as he was the person who led me in my confession of Jesus as Lord.

OH, HAPPY DAY

Mere words cannot express the changes that took place in my life as the result of my conversion. I had been translated from Islam's darkness, where no one really experientially knows God on a personal level, into a living relationship wherein I knew that God loved me and enjoyed me as a person. All the teachings of the imams, my father and grandfather, and fasting during *Ramadan* and mourning during Islamic ceremonies, never enabled me to know that God loved me and had forgiven me of my sins. That one prayer of calling on the name of Jesus for salvation satisfied my longings in a manner that all my Muslim observances never did. In a single moment, it satisfied my deep yearnings for a two-way relationship with my Creator. The Thursday night meetings took on a new dynamic for me, as I was now a full-fledged worshipper. The fact that there were other believers with whom I could fellowship was very meaningful and essential for my growth as a Christian. I regularly contacted Pastor Soodmand by phone and he patiently encouraged me and answered all of my questions. Within several months, I had read the Bible multiple times and had become competent to answer other's questions about my faith. It was ecstatic for me to have the confidence that at last I was growing spiritually by leaps and bounds. None of these things would have occurred had I not had the love and companionship of Monir, the Thursday meeting folks, and Pastor Soodmand's council. They all complied beautifully with the Lord's command of John 13:34 - *A new commandment I give to you, that you love one another; as I have loved you, that you also love one another.* What a delight it was to read my Bible in Persian rather than to continually feel the obligation to stumble through the Arabic Koran.

SUCCESS AND SUITORS

My newfound faith enhanced my educational pursuits. I had always been an excellent student, but the Lord enabled me to achieve the highest of scores on all of my final exams. Though I was only seventeen and the other girls tested were at least eighteen, I also easily passed the mandatory entrance exam for Tehran University with flying colors. My parents and all of my relatives were very proud of my scholastic achievements and presented me with expensive gifts upon my graduation from high school. Simultaneous with all this excitement, suitors began to request permission from my father to seek my hand in marriage.

In Islamic societies girls are eligible to marry as early as the age of nine. Most marry when they are in their teens without graduating from high school. In wealthy, sophisticated families, daughters are commonly given in marriage subsequent to their graduations. That had been the case with my older sisters. All through my teens suitors had come knocking at our door. Some were handsome and others, though they were exemplary in character, were hard to envision as marriage partners. They came from all levels of Iranian society and varied substantially in their respective ages and measures of wealth. One of them was the son of the one of the most famous ayatollahs in Iran.

His father's name is currently regularly highlighted on news broadcasts. For security reasons I will refrain from mentioning his name. Another potential suitor was a forty-year-old political diplomat to a European nation. All of them were well educated and most of them were from affluent families like mine.

They needed to be wealthy because my father would insist upon a large marriage dowry. The financial figure of the dowry is written into the engagement contract and deposited with the father of the bride prior to the marriage. It is always paid in cash or in gold currency. This custom is actually a protection for the woman in the event of a divorce. Divorces are rare. If a wife initiates it, her family must return the dowry. If her husband takes the initiative, the divorcee can use it for her financial sustenance.

Regardless of the various suitors' qualifications, my father refused them all. I was his youngest child and he did not fancy the idea of my leaving our home at an early age. It was his stated desire that when I did marry that my husband and I would live in the family's spacious home until we were well established in our careers. Unbeknownst to us all, the Lord had someone unique in mind for me who would overcome all of my Father's reservations.

THAT WONDERFUL LIBRARY

After the winter of my conversion, the signs of spring arrived. Everything was blooming and the migratory birds were returning from their winter retreats. Life was good. I had a vital relationship with Jesus, a good Christian support group, and my parents had made no further mention of the Bible incident. One evening I returned to the university library to complete the paper work needed for my entrance into the university. My father planned to pick me up after he had finished his teaching tasks for the day. In accordance with Islam's rulings I was properly veiled, with only my face showing, while in public. As I took my seat in the library, I could not help noticing an unusually handsome and tall young man. I also noticed that even though he appeared to be studying the book in his hand the real object of his study was none other than me. I nervously changed my seat. I did not want to violate Muslim regulations by appearing flirtatious.

Several days later it became evident that changing my seat had not discouraged him from making inquiries about me. He had discovered my name, my father's station at the university and our home address. He had gone home and asked his father to secure permission for them to visit my home. Curiously, my father had not rejected this overture like he had dozens of others like it. One fateful night the doorbell rang and there he and his father stood. Their mission was to ask my father for permission for the son to court me. His father politely introduced his son, Javid, to the family and offered his qualifications and told the story of how he had first noticed me and had come to desire to get to know me better.

According to Islamic protocol, I was not present at this first meeting. I would not be allowed to meet the young man face to face unless our families mutually agreed to the terms of the courtship and marriage. My father had not insisted that my sisters marry men that were not appealing to them. He did insist that their prospective husbands meet all of his socioeconomic expectations and his irrevocable demand that they be ardent Muslims. Javid met all of the necessary criteria. He was from a strict Muslim home, his family was affluent, and he had a bright future. After a lively discussion about the terms of the courtship and marriage my father reluctantly agreed to let things proceed to the second step.

One night just as I was settling in for my secret Bible reading session my father came to my room to speak with me. "There is a handsome fellow named Javid who saw you at the university library. We have met his family and they are requesting a second meeting to see if you are agreeable to the prospects of having him pursue you in marriage. I personally like him. He seems to be a truthful man who does not mince words. He forthrightly told me about where he first noticed you and that he felt compelled to make inquiries about you and our family. How does this sound to you?"

While my father spoke, I instinctively remembered the good-looking guy that had stared at me in the library. Something alerted me to a hint that God might be at work and I whole-heartedly agreed to meet him and his family. In my heart I believed that as a convert it would be best that I married a young man rather than an older man who was fanatical about Islam. My thought was that it would be easier to discuss spiritual matters with a younger husband.

His entire entourage arrived at our home on a beautiful Thursday evening that spring. I intently looked at my future mother- and father-in-law. Again I found myself captivated by the kind eyes of the grand fellow that I had caught looking at me in the library. I pretended that it was the first time that I had ever met him and greeted him shyly. My heart was pounding in anticipation as we both listened to the discussion about the issues of our marriage. Finally, after a bit of customary squabbling, the families came to terms about everything. Even my father appeared amicable to everything. His one unalterable command was that I was never to leave Iran for more than a vacation. My dowry was set at 2,000 gold coins. Then the exciting days of choosing a mullah to perform the ceremony and the date and place of the celebration began.

The pageantry of Iranian weddings

Like most weddings of wealthy Iranian girls, my wedding would take place at the family estate. The wedding invitations are sent to the family members of the bride and groom and the closest friends of the respective immediate families. The guests arrive dressed in their finest clothes bearing gifts that are usually quite expensive. Servants welcome them to the home and escort them to the garden or ballroom wedding site. At the appointed time a prestigious mullah signals that it is time to begin the ceremony. The bride enters with an exquisite traditional bridal gown and an ornate hijab. Special verses from the

Koran are emphasized as the mullah performing the ceremony charges the bride and groom about the responsibilities of marriage and asks them to repeat their wedding vows. After the wedding the mullah presents the couple with a beautifully handwritten copy of their marriage contract. The wedding culminates with a grand feast consisting of every form of Iranian delicacies for the guests to enjoy. Throughout the function gifted musicians play traditional Iranian songs that speak of love and celebrate marriage.

GOD IS A MATCHMAKER

Inwardly I was puzzled by what could have caused my father to consent to my marriage at an early age. He and my brothers later had second thoughts and threatened to cancel everything. However, something brought them to their senses and the plans continued smoothly on schedule. My mother had expressed fondness for Javid from the beginning. I believe that she was somewhat relieved that I was marrying a good Muslim rather than a fanatical extremist whose existence revolved around adherence to the *Sharia*. In retrospect, I now know of a certainty that the Holy Spirit was guiding every aspect of the matter.

Soon after the engagement I wanted to go to the Monday night meeting, rather than the Thursday night meeting, to share the news with my Christian friends. Above all, I wanted Pastor Soodmand to agree with me in prayer about the upcoming changes that would be taking place in my life and circumstances. I knew that he would express understanding about my marrying a Muslim who was unaware that I had converted to Christianity. In my natural mind, I would have never had an inclination to foresee the wonder of the unexpected events that would transpire that night at the meeting. I now know from personal experience that God is the greatest of matchmakers.

I excitedly entered the room and was immediately caught-up in what I would have otherwise thought was only a wishful dream. Right before my eyes sat my future husband, Javid, whom I was to marry in four days. In shock, I was tempted to pinch myself to gain the assurance that I was not in the midst of a dream while asleep in my bed at home. The thoughts that raced through my mind might seem bizarre for those who live in free societies. However, they were reasonable for someone like myself who had to keep my faith in Christ secret. Why was he in attendance at the meeting that particular night? Was he stalking me to make sure that I was really an upright Muslim girl? Had my father confided in him about my interests in the dreaded Bible and hired him to follow me? My mind raced with negative emotions. Was I going to be subjected to the embarrassment of having him publicly cancel the wedding because I was an apostate from Islam? Maybe he would cruelly keep the marriage plans intact and sentence me to a life of having to put up with his and my family's tirades about my Christianity.

As the thoughts swirled through my mind, Javid stood to his feet and approached me. At that moment, I'm now sure that the quizzical expressions on our faces matched. I was so distracted that I could not hear the questions that he was asking. "What are you doing here?" His eyes shined with questions and his face reflected shock and awe. Again he queried, "What are you doing here?"

Knowing that I was among Christian friends and that God would uphold me, I cast caution aside and boldly shot a question at him. It no longer mattered to me that as a woman in a fanatical Islamic culture my answer could likely put my very life in peril. Little did I know that he too was casting His cautions at the feet of the Lord's mercies.

"What are you doing here yourself?"

Instantly, my apprehensions began to abate as I caught the glimpse of the twinkle in his eyes. His kind smile filled me with hope, "Mina, I believe in Jesus Christ!" Then with even more conviction he loudly announced, "Yes, I believe in Jesus Christ!"

I gasped and loudly proclaimed, "Javid, I too believe that Jesus is my Savior and Lord!" Our short encounter was so loud that everyone in the room stopped chattering and fixed their eyes upon us.

Pastor Soodmand crossed the room and asked us, "Do you two know one another?"

Simultaneously, we both blurted, "We are getting married in four days."

"You both had told me that you were getting married. When I saw you speaking with one another, I was inwardly praying for your respective future mates. I had no idea that I was actually praying for both of you!"

The whole room exploded with the high praises of God. The pastor encircled us in his affectionate embrace. The tears streamed down his face as he extolled the graces of God's infinite wisdom and care. Lifting his smiling face heavenward he prayed. "Lord, nothing is ever lost from Your hands, we commit their future to you."

The meeting's agenda was transformed into a celebration for our upcoming marriage. Everyone hugged us and offered their best wishes and assured us of their continuing prayers. We barley escaped breaking Islamic tradition by hugging one another at that moment. We were able to contain ourselves from so much as holding hands, because Muslim proprieties for unmarried people still ran deeply within us. We were both grateful that we no longer had to withhold the secret of our mutual miracle salvation experiences one from another. We were ecstatic to know that God the Matchmaker had crowned us with His attestation for our relationship. No one could imagine the joy I felt as I later watched my intended spouse kneeling in prayer and offering God thanks for allowing him to have me as his bride. Few people who are born in free Western countries can realize the uniqueness of the miracle that we experienced as two young people from fanatical Muslim families. It is unheard of for a couple that know nothing of one another's secret faith to discover that they are engaged while each is posing as a Muslim.

JAVID'S MIRACLE CONVERSION

The days progressed toward the ceremony of our union and we learned much more about one another. I had not met Javid previously because he had attended the Monday night meetings rather than the Thursday night meetings that I attended. He told me of his conversion to Christ one day while we were on an errand to check on the floral arrangements for the wedding.

I was filled with the awesomeness of God's grace as he related his testimony: "Mina, my entrance into university coincided with the initiation of that horrendous war between Iraq and Iran. As you remember, all able-bodied young men were drafted into the military for a minimum of two years. I wanted no part of that war. However, had I refused to go, it would have cost me my rights to own a car, buy a home, get a university education and secure legal employment anywhere in the nation. They called me up during one of the most crucial points of the conflict. My group was given only 28 days of basic training, rather than the customary three months, and then they sent us to the frontlines. Actually they had lied to us. We were told that we would be stationed at the holy city of Meshhad and the next thing I knew, I was in the heat of the battle at the border in Basra.

"One night an Iraqi attack reduced my basic training group from 123 to 3. I was one of the three survivors and the rest were either killed or missing in action. Frankly, I feared for my life and I asked my buddies to cover for me while I took an unauthorized 48-hour leave of absence. Something within me was telling me that I needed to go and pray at the shrine of the famous imam, *Reza*, in Meshhad. The trip was almost as nerve-wracking as the battle that I had just experienced, because the fear of being caught AWOL haunted me. I hitched rides on every form of transportation from trains through army trucks and donkeys. Upon my arrival at the shrine, I forced my way through the other worshippers who were attempting to touch the edifice of gold.

"I wanted to pray like those around me, but I could not utter a word. It was as though an unseen hand was covering my mouth and smothering my words. It was alarmingly strange that I had risked my life to come and pray and my every attempt to do so failed. Inwardly I pondered about what could be happening to me. While I was in the midst of thinking, I heard a voice. I had never had such an experience previously. The voice was gentle, yet strong. 'Look at this shrine! What do you see?' I heard myself saying, 'The tomb of a dead imam.'

"The voice continued, 'Are you asking a dead man to protect your life? Ask Me, for I am your living God. Call upon my name.'

"I then felt the unseen hand releasing its grip from my lips. Not knowing how to respond, I looked toward heaven and cried out, 'God help me, I'm too young to die in this war.' After that prayer, I sensed that God was telling me that I could not spend another moment in that shrine, so I started making my way toward the exit. It was though the crowd of milling worshippers was serving as God's supernatural wave to push me out the doorway. I was tired and hungry and I decided to lookup an old friend that lived in Meshhad.

"It was a struggle to find his home, and I was ever conscious that I would shortly have to head back to the frontlines. He warmly welcomed me and invited me in for lunch. After our meal he inquired if I would like to accompany him as he went to pray, and I agreed. We drove for about an hour and a half into a rural area. When we entered the large, older home, there was a tender-faced man speaking to nearly 60 people. Many were seated on the floor and others were in chairs. The speaker, whom everyone called pastor, halted his talk and welcomed us. He happened to be Hossein Soodmand, the very pastor that blessed us the other night at the prayer meeting. Surprisingly, he greeted me with a hug and a kiss as though he had known me for years. Someone quickly shut the door and cautioned everyone to speak softly. Therefore, I surmised that I had just entered my first secret meeting, but I didn't have a clue about its purpose.

"The pastor asked my buddy to open with prayer and then everyone started singing choruses as two other fellows played guitars. The music ceased and the pastor announced that he was going to preach to us. Just before he started his address, he asked that those who had been keeping watch outside come in so they could hear what he had to say. His sermon was very different and far more comforting than anything that I had ever heard. I was deeply touched by the manner in which he explained the various trials of life that everyone experiences. At the conclusion of his talk a vibrant prayer was offered in the name of Jesus.

"While the other participants enjoyed fellowship, the pastor came over and took a seat next to me. He informed me that my friend had told him that I had just come from the frontlines of the battle in Basra. His expression was tearful as he spoke about the soldiers who were traumatized by the war and stated his sympathies for all of those who had lost loved ones in it. I knew that he was a man who sincerely cared for people and that he understood what I had been going through. Everything about him inspired me to desire to know more about the Jesus that he worshipped. I showed him a photograph of myself in my army uniform. I wanted to impress him that even though I had been fearful, I was nonetheless a disciplined soldier. As he stared at it, he put his hand on my shoulder and spoke prophetically of my future, 'You will one day become a bold, strong soldier in the army of God.'

"'Please sir, tell me what you mean by that, I really don't understand.'

"'Javid, in due time the Lord will tell you what it means.'

"Before we left to go back to Meshhad, Pastor Soodmand prayed for God's protection over my life. He added that it might not be safe or wise for me to return to Basra that night. My friend persuaded me to spend the night at his home and we talked about the things of the Lord deep into the night. I was amazed by the story of his conversion from Islam to Christianity. The miracles that he had experienced through the power of the Holy Spirit far surpassed those of the legendary Muslim heroes that I had heard about.

"Everything that happened on that trip of destiny made a lasting impression on me. My customary smile, that had vanished when I was drafted for the war, returned. It was accompanied by an inner sense of joyful peace for which I had no explanation. I wondered where it came from and could only guess that somehow it was connected to the prayers that Pastor Soodmand had offered on my behalf. His prayer for my protection was definitely effective for the remaining two years of the war. My comrades fell all around me, but I never was harmed. The scenes of that needless war that took the lives of so many of our nation's finest young men still linger with me.

"There was an eleven-year-old Iranian boy that had been critically wounded in the chest. When I passed by him he grabbed my leg and his eyes begged me for help. I picked him up like I would my own little brother and comforted him by holding my face next to his as I carried him to the hospital tent. The doctors examined him briefly and indicated that there was nothing that could be done for him. They told me that I could not remain in the tent. The little boy and I were both crying. I think that he knew from my eyes that he had my heart and love. As I turned to give him one last glance, I saw him die in the midst of one of his own cries of pain.

"All through that war the prophetic words of the pastor sustained me: 'You will one day become a bold, strong soldier in the army of God.' He had promised to continually pray for me and they were so powerful that I came to believe that the Lord and His holy angels were watching over me. God is so kind. Even though I was still a practicing Muslim, He blessed me with His protection through each day of the horrid difficulties of war.

"My joy remained, but I grew tired of holding a gun, the constant noises of battle and the stench of death. I longed to see my family and friends. Most of all I wished for another opportunity to meet with pastor Soodmand and his Christian friends. Finally, after two painfully unforgettable years, the war ended for me and I bade my soldier buddies farewell and turned toward home. Two other soldiers who had been discharged accompanied me in the jeep that sped us away from the frontline's sounds of war. I wept for my comrades that remained behind and wished for their safety. My excitement of being back in Tehran and resuming my studies at the university soon overshadowed my memories of the prayer meeting, God's hand of protection and the kind pastor. My mind was caught up in the world of my studies and part-time work, until Pastor Soodmand phoned and made me a most unusual offer.

"He had heard that I had returned to Tehran and telephoned me countless times to invite me to the meetings. I used every excuse, including lies, to avoid going. One fateful day he called and announced that he was coming to visit me at my place of employment. He asked how much I earned each month and said that if I would attend a two-hour meeting he would give an entire month's salary. I was out of excuses and lies. I refused his offer for the money, but agreed to follow him to the meeting.

"I had mixed emotions about the meeting. Perhaps even more than my first encounter with the group, the fellowship, the music and his preaching touched something within me. However, I was on my way to a good life and had no interest in complicating things by getting involved in what I had always been taught was a false religion. While the others fellowshipped and enjoyed refreshments after the meeting, Pastor Soodmand again came and seated himself beside me. He issued a decree that shocked me to my core. I winced with questions as he put his hand on my shoulder. 'Tonight, the Lord has put it on my heart to become your shadow. Until the morning, I'm going to follow you everywhere that you go. If you attempt to lose me, my face will be the first thing that you see when you come out of your house tomorrow. If you go to the university, I'll be there. If you try to elude me by climbing a mountain peak, I'll meet you at its top. You will find no city of refuge that lacks my presence.'

"I responded with an expression that conveyed the absence of understanding and quite a bit of dismay, 'I'm going home, if you choose to follow me you are welcome to do so.' He made his promise sure and he and two other fellows followed me to my residence. Fortunately, upon my arrival home I found a note from my mother stating that the family would be away visiting relatives. I invited the guys in and politely offered to fix them something to eat. One of them told me that it was far more important that I take advantage of the opportunity to spend time with the man of God and that he and his friend would take care of fixing the food. Pastor Soodmand spoke to me about the glories of Jesus for three hours straight. I intermittently spat out rebuttals comprised of classic Islamic objections to Christianity. Inwardly, considering all that God had done for me during the war, I shocked myself with the intensity of my rebellious objections.

"He told me that Jesus was present with us and that He would grant any of my heart's desires that I asked for in His name. At 2:00 in the morning, with final exasperation, I declared that I would not believe anything about Jesus unless God gave me a specific supernatural sign. This did not flutter the minister one iota. He shook my hand and promised that the Lord would do whatever I requested, because He had all the powers available in heaven and earth. I assured him that regardless of my respect for him, I thought that he was deceived by a lie. I added that if I were given a divine sign, I would immediately confess Jesus as my Lord. He responded by reading a single verse from the Bible and then he led us in a prayer that beseeched the Lord to give me a sign. The verse was John 20:29 — *Jesus said to him, 'Thomas, because you have seen Me, you have believed. Blessed are those who have not seen and yet have believed.'*

"The next thing that happened was truly miraculous. My spirit was translated into the invisible spiritual dimension of God. I could not speak or feel my own body. I was simply alone in some unknown eternal region. The awesome sense of a holy presence pulsated through my entire being. Suddenly, a loving voice called my name. It had the familiar sound of the one that I had heard two years previously in Meshhad. 'Javid! Javid! Are you putting Me to a test that I must pass or is it I who must test you? I am the Lord. Don't tread on areas of authority that belong solely to Me.' Those words resounded in my ears and every sin that I had ever committed emerged into my thoughts. I heard the pastor reading the verse as my sins passed before me like a shameful video that was exposed by the holiness of Christ.

"I knew that my sign had been granted without the necessity of seeing Him. Hearing His voice was sufficient for me to immediately make the decision to devote my life to Him. Making that life-transforming decision caused my spirit to awaken to the temporal realm. My first conscious experience was hearing the pages of the pastor's Bible rustle as he looked for other verses. He started reading verses to me and I stared at him and asked that he hush. He took on a solemn demeanor and began to apologize for upsetting me. I interrupted him with my confession of Jesus as my Lord. I loudly wailed for the world to hear, 'You have read enough. At this moment, I believe in Jesus more than you do.'

"I was unaware that my hands were lifted in homage to Jesus as I cried forth my declaration. Pastor Soodmand began to leap into the air and to shout hallelujah praises. His Bible sailed toward the ceiling as he shouted, 'Hallelujah, hallelujah, I told you that you would become one of His soldiers!' The two other guys bounded from the kitchen and I asked them if they had any idea what had just happened.

"'Of course we do. It doesn't take four hours to cook eggs. We have been in there praying for you the whole time and we know that God answers prayers. Our prayer was that God would open your eyes to the truth.'

"I explained that they could leave with the confidence that their mission had been accomplished. I did not want them to risk discovery if my Muslim parents arrived home unexpectedly. I continued by telling them that I was willing to repent in the street if necessary. The pastor laid his hand upon me and led me in a prayer of repentance. At its conclusion he gave me another prophetic word. 'Javid, God wants to bless you with a special gift, but I'm not sure what it might be.' I requested that he pray for me in any manner that he liked. I can still sense the feelings of the anointing that came upon me as he prayed. Subsequently there have been many infallible proofs that the Lord graced me with the gift of evangelism that night."

NEW LIFE

Our wedding ceremony incorporated all the pageantry of high society Iranian weddings. The guest list was restricted to family members and only the closest of friends. Pastor Soodmand had advised Javid and me of an ingenious way in which to override the Koranic verses that were to be cited in the ceremony. We uttered the name of Jesus under our breath as the imam spoke forth each verse. The Muslims thought it was a typical wedding. We knew that God's only begotten Son had officiated at our wedding.

Even though Father gave us the title to our own apartment as a wedding gift, he insisted that we move into his home until we got established. Javid needed to complete his university degree and to find employment that was commensurate with his skills. Then there was the matter of our saving the funds necessary to setup housekeeping for ourselves. By the grace of God Javid and I were able to keep our faith in Christ a secret. Had we been discovered we might have been turned over to the authorities. They would attempt to force us to recant our faith. These ruthless servants of Allah would have no qualms about torturing us to get the results that they desired. Worse still, it would not be unusual for our respective parents to murder us for embarrassing their families by becoming apostates from Islam. None of the possibilities for impending doom hindered our devotion to Jesus and to one another. Our private devotional times as a couple frequently featured thanksgivings to

God for bringing us together. It soon became apparent that Javid's spiritual gift that Pastor Soodmand had prophesied was that of an evangelist. Together we saw many Muslims renounce their beliefs and embrace the cross of Christ. This burden and gifting has never waned from our lives.

One of Javid's first substantial job offers required that he work in an oil company located in the southern Iranian city of Abadan for one year. During that period I could visit him from time to time, but it would be inconvenient for us to pickup and move there. At first he was tempted to reject the offer and then we decided that it was a good career move for him to accept it. This began a nomadic period in our lives that lasted for years. First due to his employment, and later because our conversions became known, the initial years of our married life involved moving from city to city, country to country. Much to my disappointment, I was never the mistress of my own household in my hometown of Tehran.

In spite of the threat that our Christianity might be revealed, and our frequent job-related separations, we were happy. Perhaps one of the most enjoyable seasons of our early marriage was the celebration of *Norooz*, the Iranian New Year that begins on March the 19th. Its festivities have few equals anywhere in the world. My mother made the preparations for the New Year special in every respect. Exquisite floral arrangements decorated the house and delightful chocolates, nuts, dried fruits, and pastry goodies were displayed throughout our home. During the day of the first night's celebration mother spent the entire time cooking. She loved to see her massive family gathered to enjoy the dishes she had prepared. We relished her *sabazi polo* on a bed of basmati rice mixed with special herbs and saffron. She added salmon with fresh-squeezed lemon juice as a decorative and tasty side dish.

Father also played a part in the festivities. He would insert ten thousand Iranian Rial bank notes into his Koran. The legend was that this empowered the money with a special blessing. All of the guests also brought notable gifts for those in attendance. Some brought jewelry and others expensive clothing. My father really enjoyed distributing the money from his Koran to my brothers and the rest of the family. Of course, we all looked forward to his presentations.

When Javid was away I would relax on the couch and enjoy the spring scenery from my favorite living room window. The birds would sing and I could see the goldfish surfacing in our garden pond. This period was reminiscent of the peaceful days of my early childhood when my youngest brother and I would stuff ourselves with the New Year's delicacies as we watched television programs. It was a great joke for my mother to tease us about the volumes of food that we devoured. I will never forget my mother's happy smiles and the sunshiny days that were filled with sweet fragrances of Iranian roses. In those early days of my marriage, how could I suspect that our entire world was about to undergo tragic, life-altering events?

Chapter 3

COMFORT IN THE VALLEY OF DARKNESS

BAPTISMAL JOYS

Monir increasingly became a strong support for me in the early days of my marriage. She had rejected her many qualified suitors because she wanted to devote her energies to her work for the Lord. Winning souls was her life and, for her, time was of the essence. She felt that the coming of the Lord was at hand and that many Muslims needed to find the Lord through the materials that she placed in strategic places. She laughed when Pastor Soodmand referred to her as the official Bible and tract distributor for Tehran.

I became very excited when Monir told me that there was to be a water baptism celebration for six of those who had recently been converted. It was to take place the next evening and I was one of the six candidates who were to follow the Lord's command of Acts 2:38 - *Then Peter said to them, "Repent, and let every one of you be baptized in the name of Jesus Christ for the remission of sins; and you shall receive the gift of the Holy Spirit."* Pastor Soodmand was to officiate and the bathtub of the apartment in which the meetings were held was to be our baptismal font. It could have been in a grand cathedral, a river, or a bathtub, for me the important thing was that it was obedience to my Lord.

Monir was concerned that I might experience some difficulties in getting to the meeting the following night, so she spent the night in our home. That afternoon we sat on the treasured Persian rug that my grandfather had given me as a birthday gift the year prior to his death and talked. Just before sundown we took a walk in the nearby forest. It was wonderful to be surrounded by God's creation. It was though His voice beckoned to us from the breeze that gently touched the colorful plant life around us. We decided to build a small fire and spread a small linen cloth to sit upon. Monir pointed to a lovely butterfly that came to rest beside us. Perhaps it wanted a front row seat as we spoke of its Creator and worshipped Him. Monir softly hummed the melody of her favorite song that is titled, *He is Lord.* We sang together, "*He has risen from the dead and He is Lord. Every knee shall bow and every tongue shall confess that Jesus Christ is Lord.*"

The fire had an unusual glow and its smoke drifted in wisps through the trees. It seemed that it was hoping for its final release into the sky. It spoke to me of the Lord who is the greatest of all who rise. He releases all who find Him into a new world of love, mercy and forgiveness. Monir and I prayed together and she took on a rather solemn demeanor. She explained that Satan often attempts to disrupt the joy of people's baptisms by causing problems. He hates the truths that this sacrament represents. It is a signal that everything of one's old life is buried. It has a special significance for Muslims because it drowns the bondages of Islam and the *Sharia* laws with finality. That is exactly what I was looking forward to. I had taken steps toward the light and wanted to be completely freed from the powers of that dark religion.

We returned to the house and continued to talk late into the night. We were sitting on the same Persian rug that my grandfather had given me as a birthday gift the year prior to his death. Inwardly I was musing over some rather heavy thoughts. Everything that happens in life does so with purpose. The Lord can intermingle His thoughts with ours to give us hints of what the future holds. Monir fell into line with my thoughts. She spoke of the many trials that she had gone through over the eight years since her conversion and added that she had always felt the Lord beside her. Then she began to speak of the fact that sometimes believers must give their lives for the faith. She punctuated that it was especially true in Islamic nations. I told her that I was thirsty for God's presence no matter what the costs. She lifted her hands upward and encouraged me to tell the Lord what I desired.

Without waking the household, I prayed as loudly as I could. "Lord for 17 years I was on a spiritual path that was not of my choosing. I've got no desire to be a Muslim like all of my ancestors. I need more of You. Show me more of Yourself and Your ways. I will serve You forever." While I was praying Monir turned to John 8:12 – *Then Jesus spoke to them again, saying, "I am the light of the world. He who follows Me shall not walk in darkness, but have the light of life."*

GLIMPSES INTO THE FUTURE

Tomorrow was to be the big day. I, along with five others including a girl that Monir had won to Christ, was to be baptized. She planned to deliver some books to the university and was to be back by early afternoon. We wanted plenty of time to make it to Ali's apartment by 7:30 that evening. When I climbed into bed and turned out the light Monir was still praying. I soon fell asleep. In the midst of the night I was wakened by her cries as she prayed for me. She had not gotten any sleep, as she was so intent about praying that I would see more of the Lord's glory. She was amazing. I reminded her of the dream that I had just prior to my conversion. In it I saw Jesus and heard Him saying, "I am the way, the truth and the life." Monir's Bible was opened before her and she had been reading John 14:6 that says those very words. She came over and began to hug and kiss me, "Mina, I've never been so happy in all of my life. It will be a great victory over Satan when you are baptized tomorrow. We have to be in prayer and very wise not to give any opportunity to the evil one. I feel a little strange. About six years ago I met a sister in the Lord from Africa. She told me that she believed that I would someday be martyred for my faith." I urged her to get some sleep. Finding sleep again was difficult for me because I was concerned about her words.

MISSING ANGEL

The next morning I awoke with the same thoughts on my mind. After receiving Jesus, I had only known peace and joy, now for the first time I felt an element of fear. Monir left for the university saying that she did not feel like she could eat breakfast. I stayed home because she said that she would be back in time for lunch. My mother had a great admiration for Monir's many good qualities. When she walked out the door she asked her not to eat while away as she was fixing kebab with rice for lunch. She knew that it was her favorite dish.

The hours ticked by far past lunchtime. I told mother that we should wait for Monir to return before eating. I figured that perhaps something at the university was delaying her. I went to my room to study the Bible and to pray about my baptism that evening. I came out when I heard my mother expressing concern about Monir's delay. We both wondered where she could be. I returned to my room and began to intercede for the Lord to bring her home safely. It was close to 2:00 and normally she would have called if she were going to be delayed. I went downstairs and found mother sitting on the couch with a worried look. She asked me to go ahead and eat. I only toyed with the delicious food and mother would not eat anything. She loved Monir like one of her own daughters. She spoke of the possibility that she had been in an accident or something. I was also secretly concerned that I might not make it to the baptism that night. It would be awful if she missed witnessing the occasion that we so honored. Mother mentioned that it was possible that she had decided to go to her own home before coming back for lunch and that perhaps we should telephone for her. I didn't think that was possible in light of our plans for the evening. I told mother that we were going to visit a mutual friend that night and that she had promised to come back and get me. At

4:30 mother called her house and they said that they assumed that she was with us.

Her father expressed immediate worry for her safety. We told him that she had gone to deliver some books to the university and he questioned what type they were. He told us that he had warned her about going to the university after hours and again asked where she had gone. "My daughter is a punctual girl and she is conscientious about calling us if she is going to be late."

As he was speaking with us by phone, my father walked into the house. I cringed with apprehension when he saw our distress and asked what was happening. I regretted that we had telephoned her house. If my father discovered our Christianity it would be devastating for all concerned. He inquired about the possibility that we could go to her home and assist her parents in trying to locate her. By then the time to leave for the baptismal service had passed and I went in to the yard to secretly telephone Ali. I was heartsick that I had to tell him that I was going to miss the meeting in his home. I also wanted to ask him if he had heard anything from Monir. From the house I heard my father's complaints that the phone always got lost when he needed it the most. He wanted to start calling the hospitals in an effort to locate Monir. I quickly dialed Ali's number. Initially it was busy, but on the second try he answered my call. The Lord had answered my prayer that I would get through before father exploded with anger.

"Where are you guys?" It was apparent that he knew nothing about my friend's whereabouts. I told him about her and the whole group in his apartment began to intercede about the situation. Pastor Soodmand took the phone from him and I rapidly told him everything. He was greatly disturbed.

I was relieved that he and the group were aware of what was happening. I had the confidence that they would do what was needed: pray. I ran to the house and put the phone on the couch. Monir's parents and her brother had arrived. I greeted them, but they made no response due to their concerns for their missing sister and daughter. Her mother was crying and mine was attempting to comfort her. My father found the phone and became frustrated that it had been left on the couch. My brother-in-law took the phone and began to call every imaginable place.

He angrily asked, "Where is she? The people at the university didn't see her today and the police have no ideas about where she is. She is not in any of the hospitals. Where is that girl?" His father paced the floor with his cell phone in hand and would not speak to anyone.

I peeked out the door hoping to see her approaching the house. My father shouted at me, "Where do you think you are going? Shut that door you are not going anywhere." No one listened to my explanation about why I was looking out the door. They were far too upset to pay any attention to me. Monir's middle brother arrived on the scene. He was one of Tehran's most respected judges. His face was flushed with anger. He didn't say anything at first, but it was obvious that he knew something that we didn't. We all looked at him in anticipation as he walked over and grasped his father's hands,

BAPTISM OF TEARS

"The execution office has arrested Monir and she is being detained in Evin prison."

Her mother fainted and everyone else began to spit questions at him, "Why? What are the charges?" He shook his head and told us that he didn't know why she was arrested. Instinctively, I knew that they must have caught her in possession of Christian material. In Iran that charge carries the death sentence for Muslims. They are often brutally tortured before they are executed. The conversation that we had about the devil's disruptions when people want to be baptized and the premonition of the African woman about her being martyred loomed into my mind.

The Evin prison has a terrible history. The Shah of Iran, its former king, had built it as the house of incarceration for political prisoners. Few people that went in made it out alive. All were tortured and most were executed. Islam is a political religion. My dear Monir was being held, and likely being beaten, for apostasy from Islam. I could no longer selfishly think about missing my baptismal service, it was time to really pray for her life.

The judge left to check on her at the prison. While he was gone, my father told Monir's that there must have been a mistake. He stated that he intended to make the silly people that would arrest a good Muslim girl like Monir pay for their foolishness. Her own father silently stared at the floor. I knew that there had been no mistake and that she had been arrested because of her allegiance to King Jesus.

As I went to my room to pray, I heard Monir's mother assuring everyone that her son the judge could get her daughter out of any mess, "You wait and see. They will both come walking though that door. My son will surely use his official powers to free her from that terribly scary place." My room became a prayer sanctuary as I alternated between intercession and worry about her physical welfare. Floggings and rape were routine experiences for those charged with Monir's alleged crime. My thoughts of what she might be going through were terrifying. I called for her release in the authority of the name of Jesus just like Pastor Soodmand had taught us.

I mustered every ounce of faith within me in my prayers for victory. Everyone's face was drawn with anxiety. I wished that it was possible to tell them what had happened and that they would miraculously agree with me in prayer for her release. It was a fruitless wish. My Muslim relatives were so fanatical that they would have temporarily been more outraged by my Christianity than they were worried about Monir's imprisonment. No one that has not been in my situation can know what I was going through. Christians of the West simply do not have the experience of knowing what it is like to live under the shadow of persecution in an Islamic nation.

Intermittently, as I interceded in my room, I wondered if I was praying the right way. Each time that doubt came into my mind I relied on my knowledge of the Bible. My God was not like Muhammad's Allah. He does not demand that anyone must ritualistically pull out a prayer rug and spout prayers in a specific language that they do not fully understand. It was comforting to know that He knew my heart and would hear me regardless of the particular form of Christian prayer that I might choose to use. While in my room I came upon a piece of paper that had something written on it that looked like Monir's handwriting. It was one of the Bible verses that she had written out for me to memorize. My sobs were so intense that the muscles of my throat ached.

My mother called me to the phone. It was Javid calling from his Abadan job site. When I whispered what was happening he changed the subject because he suspected that the authorities had a wiretap on our phone line. Being a Christian, he was very well acquainted with the perilous implications of the situation. He also knew that it could bring about the discovery of our secret lives. It was clear to both of us that Satan was upset about our faith in Christ and that he would try anything to discourage us. Javid expressed his desire to leave immediately for Tehran, but he had several months remaining in his contract. He gave me his love and assured me that he would be praying and said goodbye.

We were all waiting for Monir's brother to return from Evin prison and each minute that passed seemed like days. He had been gone for at least three hours. I went downstairs to get some cold water just as he was coming through the door. Monir's mother's predication that he would return with his sister was not fulfilled. I stood in the doorway of the kitchen to hear what he had to say as he spoke with those in the living room. He did not look good and he shook his head negatively when he was asked if she was sitting in the car. He slouched sullenly in my father's armchair and then angrily pounded the Koran's sacred table so hard that it fell to the floor. My mother ran and picked it up and kissed it before replacing it on the table. He said one word, *Kafar*. It conveyed the worst thing that could be said of a Muslim. It meant that they were infidels, non-believers and guilty of denying Allah. He then apologized to my father for insulting the Koran and lifted it to his lips and kissed it. Were it not for the grievousness of the circumstances my father would have thrown him out of the house.

THEY MURDERED MONIR

Monir's mother began to pound herself and wail, "Why? Why, my daughter? Allah kill me, just let me die." No one could calm her screams. The judge promised her that he would do everything in his power to get her out on bail and since the hour was late, my parents insisted that everyone spend the night in our home. That which I was experiencing during that 24-hour time slot was the nightmare of my life. I really wanted to telephone the pastor and feared for my own safety if I was caught in the act. I was fully aware that the life of my dear Javid and myself was on the brink of monumental changes.

That night as I made my way up the stairs to get some sleep, I heard father speaking with mother. He instructed her that I was not to be out of her sight until the whole matter was resolved. He was concerned that something might also befall me. I got out my Bible and found that Monir had tucked one of her typical notes of encouragement in its pages. It directed me to Col. 3:13-14 - *bearing with one another, and forgiving one another, if anyone has a complaint against another; even as Christ forgave you, so you also must do. [14] But above all these things put on love, which is the bond of perfection.*

The following day, Mother and I accompanied Monir's mother to her home as a demonstration of our love and support. All that day we all struggled with our understanding of Evin prison's reputation. Anyone that was not released after a few days was never again to be seen alive by his or her family. For the whole time that we were there in her home, Monir's mother wailed in the emotion-filled Middle Eastern style. The sound of it echoes in my ears to this day. Later that night, after we arrived home, I made the decision to risk everything by calling Pastor Soodmand in Meshhad. It was well past midnight and there was no answer, so I called Ali's home. His wife did not answer my greeting in her customary joyful manner. She sounded aloof as though she did not want to speak with me. I urged her to let me speak with Ali and she said that he was not available. I was mystified as I hung up the receiver.

Shortly afterward, our phone rang. When I answered it, Ali's wife was on the line telling me that she was calling from a pay telephone. They were suspicious that their phone line was being tapped. I continued my conversation with her after I checked to make sure that my parents had not awakened as the phone rang. I was horrified to learn that Ali had also been arrested within a close time period of Monir's arrest. Four Islamic officials had burst into their apartment at 8:00 in the morning. Ali had just left and they ransacked the house and confiscated all of the Christian materials found in the home. Tragically, they had also found and took Ali's personal phone diary that listed everyone's numbers and names. I knew that my name and number were in the diary and that intensified my apprehensions. It could mean trouble for Javid and me and ruin my parents' reputation in Tehran's high society. I told her about Monir's situation and she promised to contact Pastor Soodmand. She had unsuccessfully attempted to reach him earlier that day. Our only hope was that which could come from the Lord who lived in our hearts.

Previous to that point, I had never been afraid to walk the streets of my hometown. Now I was afraid to venture out even in the company of my parents. I knew that the radical thugs who watched the streets for the authorities would have no qualms about taking me into custody if we were stopped and questioned in relation to our identities. That could mean imprisonment, beatings, rape and death. It all made me cringe at the thought of being approached by any stranger. My family went to Monir's home and my older sisters met us there. Her brother who was the judge looked angry and sad about the news he was about to give us. In exasperation he complained of the disgrace of having a sister who had converted to the despised religion of Christianity. He explained that he had visited her in the prison. He asked her mother if Monir had a back condition. He made the inquiry because she had been favoring her back while he spoke with her. She had winced in pain and refused his attempt to hug her when he first saw her. The bruises on her face revealed that she had been beaten. It was horrible to imagine what she must have gone through in those initial hours of incarceration.

My sister's husband turned to me and inquired if I knew anything about Monir's involvement with Christians. My heart pounded as I eked out a weak, no. "Are you sure? You two girls were the best of friends and it seems unlikely that you would not know one another's intimate secrets." I again lied, and said that I knew nothing about the matter. His eyes told me that he didn't believe me, but he didn't repeat the question.

Five days later, Monir's father came to our home and told us that she was to be released in two more days. He was confident of her release, as he had promised the authorities that she would renounce Christianity, repent for insulting Islam and return to the true faith. He said that he had been instructed to bring clean clothes and a fresh veil for the day of her freedom. That provided some temporary relief for everyone after days filled with fear that was coupled with agitation. I personally doubted that she would renounce the Lord no matter what her father promised and regardless of the amount of times that they subjected her to torture. Had her relatives not been influential people in the Islamic government, they would have killed her immediately. I pondered what I would do if I were in her situation. I hoped that I would not give in to the brutalities and renounce my Lord.

A special celebration was planned for the day of her release and several members of her family had sworn oaths to Allah if she returned home. Two days prior to her release we were watching the evening news. The broadcast's commentator was reading off the list of "seditious ones" that had been executed. It was unusual for a day to pass without someone's name being announced. This list was made up of those charged with religious and political crimes. Normally they were either shot or hung by the neck until dead. According to Islamic regulations these deeds have to be completed before sunrise. Father was in his armchair and mother was in the midst of reciting her *salat*. I was not watching the news but could hear it as I did some ironing in the living room. To the horror of us all, the fourth name announced was that of Monir Shams, my beloved friend. Mother bolted from her prayers and I was so startled that I dropped the iron on the Persian rug. The stench of the burning fibers filled the room. I picked it up the iron while keeping my eyes glued to the television. The ruthlessly radical Muslims of Iran had martyred the official Bible distributor of Tehran and the gracious daughter of God who was my spiritual confidant. The strength abated from my legs. I reeled from shock and collapsed to the floor next to the hole in the burnt carpet.

We all went through the mental gymnastics of suggesting that her name had been cited by mistake. After all, the authorities had promised the judge that she would be set free two days later. We should have known better than to trust people whose entire religion is built upon deceptions. My father, my mother, and I were well acquainted with the Islamic principle of *Al Takeyya*. It encourages Muslims to lie at anytime that they sense that it is for the betterment of Islam (Narrated by al-Bukhari, 2546; Muslim, 2605). Those people lied to us as a lesson to all Iranians of what happens to families that don't keep tight reins on their daughters. The truth is, for many Muslims, lying is as easy as breathing. If Allah absolves one of guilt, what reason is there to be concerned about the feelings of the family of the murdered? All three of us climbed into the car and sped to Monir's parents' home. From the driveway in front of their home we could hear her mother's anguished screams. The sound of her voice reverberated through the whole neighborhood. Our hopes were dashed, no mistakes had been made, Monir, had been martyred at the age of twenty-eight. I stood by the car dazed with unbelief. They had murdered her exactly 10 hours after they swore that she would be freed to rejoin her dear ones.

I felt the tug of my mother's hand as she pulled me into the house. The most gifted of writers would have difficulty describing the spectacle of her bereaved loved ones. Everyone was wearing black and even the night seemed to have taken on an especially sinister blackness. Her mother's face was stained with blood from the places where she had scratched herself. Perhaps her emotional pain was so deep that she needed to offset it by inflicting physical pain upon herself.

She took the fresh clothes and veil that she had packed for her daughter's trip home and showed them to everyone. I took the veil from her and buried my face in it. Its scent brought visions of the wonderful times of fellowship that I had enjoyed with my faithful companion. I sobbed and sunk further into the depths of grief. In contrast, other members of the clan, who were Islamic clergymen, showed no signs of sympathy. They just whispered among themselves. It was as though they believed that Monir had gotten her just punishment for rebelling against Islam. Her brother, my sister's husband, displayed a face that was wet from weeping. His precious little sister was gone forever. My own father had put his regal pride aside and sat in a corner with his face in his hands.

Fear gripped my soul and I battled nerve-wracking thoughts. The authorities had everyone's name that attended Pastor Soodmand's Tehran prayer meetings. This strongly supported the possibilities that the sobering scene that I was witnessing might soon be duplicated throughout Iran. Every parent that had adult children in Ali's phone diary might soon be dressed in mourning attire. I was attempting to fend off these fears through faith when a young girl handed me a note and quickly walked away. I made my way to the restroom and read it. "You must leave Iran immediately. Your and your husband's names are on the black list. Call 213-0579." I memorized the number and flushed the note down the toilet. I looked for the messenger among the mourners and could not find her. I had never seen her prior to that time and never saw her again. Having heard about Monir's martyrdom, Javid rushed in from his job-site abroad while I was fighting a new round of terrifying thoughts of what would befall us. He had been granted emergency leave due to the death of a loved one. I whispered to him the note's message and the number that was to be called. Instantly, I observed that his keen mind had shifted into a mode that would find us a path of escape. The Lord's light illuminated our path through the valley of death. That path led us into exile from the nation of our births over 22 long years ago.

HABITATIONS OF CRUELTY

Muslim activists who operate in the Western world beguile those who listen to them with lies. They claim that Islam is a religion of peace, tolerance and beauty. They exalt Muhammad as the last and greatest of prophets, who was a gentle man of peace. But, if his Islam is truly a religion of peace, how can his Allah command that Muslims terrorize and kill anyone who they think is against Allah? The conditions in Iran, and other Islamic countries, today are the same that they were when we went into exile. Young women who refuse to wear veils are charged with apostasy. The mullahs teach that any Muslim girl who dies while still a virgin will ascend to paradise. To ensure that the girls who are to be executed will go to hell, the guards of the prisons systematically rape them before their executions. I previously spoke of the pageantry of Iranian weddings. I failed to mention that many times the brides' ages span from 9 to 14 years of age. The grooms are often complete strangers to their little brides and grossly senior to them in age. These children's first misshaped sexual experiences are frequently nothing less than the horrors of pedophilic rape. Iran's fundamentalist Muslim regime does not tolerate the open declaration of the Gospel of Christ. Any ex-Muslim caught practicing Christianity meets the same fate that Monir did 22 years ago. The extremists who perpetrate these injustices find justification for them through the life and words of Muhammad. One of his eleven wives was a six-year-old-child. In the Koran and the Hadith he encouraged his followers to cut off the arms and legs of unbelievers on the opposite sides of their bodies (Surah 5:33). His remedy for them was to hunt them down and to slaughter them anywhere that they were found (Surah, Al Ahzab:61).

FINDING A PATH

The day after the wake, Javid had to go into the main part of the city to settle some business for our trip. We had prayed the entire night and asked the Lord to oversee everything related to our covert departure from Iran. The person that we needed to contact for our escape to safety could not merely be a travel agent that arranged vacation getaways for wealthy people on short notice. The person that we needed would have to be a specialist in smuggling people out of the nation. I phoned the number that had been on the note, and a man with a heavy Turkish accent answered. Just as I began to explain who I was and what I needed, father interrupted by demanding to know to whom I was speaking. I said it was Javid and he grabbled the phone from my hand and rudely asked the person on the line to identify himself. The phone went dead. Apparently, he had heard father's question and had wisely hung up.

"Who were you talking to?"

"Father, it was Javid, just like I told you it was."

"Girl, do you think that I'm a fool?" He was pointing to Javid's cell phone that had been accidentally left on the couch were I was sitting. "Child, these are dangerous times. You and Javid should not underestimate me. I know what is going on. I will not let you jeopardize your life for him. You were my daughter long before you were his wife. Don't you understand that the government is tapping the phone lines of everyone connected to Monir? Don't ever lie to me again."

Javid arrived home and I told him about the incident with father and the phone. Fortunately, he had made contact with the Turk while he doing his errands. The fellow had refused to discuss anything over the telephone and asked for a private rendezvous with Javid the next day. His caution helped us realize that the pressures at hand could cause us to make strategic blunders if we were not more careful.

Javid brought an encouraging report from the Turk. He was quite sure that he could easily smuggle us out of the country with two other Christians that were being forced into exile. He warned that the trip would be hazardous and that we would have to go by way of Turkey. Upon hearing this news, we knew that there was no time to ponder our options with idle contemplations, and that we had to move quickly. We soon learned that our comrades on this risky trek would be two friends from the prayer meetings, Reza and Bita. This faithful couple had come to Christ the year following Monir's conversion. Actually, Monir had introduced Bita to the Master and she in turn had introduced her husband to Him.

My sister's husband, who was Monir's brother, discerned that Javid and I were believers in Christ and that we likely attended the same Christian functions that Monir attended. He related this to my parents. I could tell from the shift in my father's attitudes toward us that he was waiting to see some evidence that would confirm my brother-in-law's suspicions. He told my sister that should he discover that Javid had any part in taking me to Christian gatherings, he would file for a divorce from him on my behalf. When she spoke to me about it, I denied everything that they were suspecting. I had to lie. I know that many Christians would raise objections to my saying this. However, they do not understand the cruel grip that Islam puts on people.

My father's esteem for *Sharia* law could have easily compelled him to either kill us himself or turn us over to the authorities. Such betrayals are commonplace within Muslim societies. The people who betray their loved ones are deceived into believing that they are doing Allah a favor. It is true enough that my parent's love for me might have caused them to be forgiving. We could not take that gamble. Flight was our only wise option. While I knew that I was deeply loved by my family, and the thought of leaving Iran was unbearable, we simply had to flee.

THE UNEXPECTED

One morning during this pivotal period of our lives, I awoke not feeling well. I assumed that all the pressures on us were taking their toll because we were to depart Iran in just four days. Mother insisted that I undergo an examination by our family's physician. His tests revealed that I was eight weeks pregnant. Mother burst into praises to Allah and immediately began to make plans for a party to celebrate this momentous occasion. She naively thought that the coming of a grandchild would override everyone's memories of what the Islamic authorities had put us through. I knew better and my mind sank into the implications of bringing forth a baby while we were trying to find a safe haven in some foreign land. I shuttered at the thought that my baby might be born as we lived as vagabonds sneaking from country to country. My only comfort was that I knew that God has a history of helping mothers deliver their baby's under less than ideal circumstances. He did it for Mary and Jesus and He could easily do the same for my baby and me.

I called Javid and he rejoiced at the news. He read my concerns through the sound of my voice and assured me that everything would be all right. Actually, I was not sure that he was really as happy as he pretended to be. How could anyone be happy about venturing for two weeks through dangerous mountain terrains with a wife who was carrying their first child? Even my father acted as though nothing was wrong. It was as though he had forgotten that there was a good possibility that we were secret Christians. He insisted we continue living in his home until after the baby arrived. It was painful to envision that my father would not be able to smile down upon his 16th grandchild right after its birth. My circle of delight over the baby and dilemma over our upcoming trip intensified.

Several days later my father presented me with a baby

stroller. My mother laughingly teased him for buying presents for a baby who was months away from delivery. My mother noticed my seriousness and inquired about it. I told her that I was still thinking about Monir and that my first pregnancy was giving me the same concerns that any first-time mother would have. She was such an angel. I really wished that we could tell my parents that we planned to leave in just a few days. Even more, I wished that we all worshipped the same God and shared the same faith in Jesus. They were such loving people, and Christianity would have made them even more so. I again tried to comfort myself. I thought that perhaps we could return to Tehran in a couple of years. I could not comprehend the fact that we would not see them again face-to-face for decades.

At one point I tried to talk Javid into staying. I asked if he really wanted me to walk through the mountains while carrying his baby in my womb. He emphatically responded, "Mina, we have two choices, departure or death." He went on to say that if we stayed we would have to renounce our faith in Christ before the Islamic council. He searched my face as he asked, "Do you think that either of us would be willing to do that?"

My emphatic answer was, "No, we could never do such a thing." I had seen Jesus in my dreams and had felt His hands on my shoulders. His glory filled rooms where I was worshipping God with dear Monir, and the Muslims had murdered her. It was unthinkable to seriously contemplate renouncing my faith. I would accompany Reza, Bita and my husband and flee, regardless of what might befall my baby and me.

DARKNESS FALLS

The Sabbath for Muslims falls on Friday, so therefore Saturday is the first day of the work week in Iran. The Saturday before we were to sneak away, Javid had gone to visit his parents. I awoke with an extreme case of pregnancy nausea. In compliance with Mother's request, I spent the day resting and reading in our room. She was very concerned that I carry my child full term and would not allow me to do anything strenuous. As usual, Father came into my room and bid his grand-child in my womb goodbye for the day, and fondly kissed my forehead. He loved children and was anxious that the nine months speed by so that he could hold the latest addition to his brood of grandchildren. Shortly after my father left for work, an authoritative knock sounded at the front door. I looked out the window and saw two armed officers from the same depart-ment of the government that had arrested Monir.

In panic, I called to Mother to get the door. She mistakenly thought that I was saying that I would answer the door and did not answer its knock right away. When they knocked more forcefully a second time, she commanded that I remain upstairs and she went down to investigate their purpose. I knew that such persons carry the authority to break into homes to arrest fugitives. I quickly gathered a few clothes and took a good sum of money from my father's cash drawer. I slipped out the back door and hid out of their sight with the door slightly ajar. I could hear them speaking with my mother. They said that they had a warrant from the prosecutor's office for my arrest. As she was pleading with them not to take me, they roughly pushed her aside and rushed in the house searching for me. I marshaled every bit of strength that I had and fled down the street. The last sounds that I ever heard from my mother's lips were her screams that they leave me alone. My last look at her face saw her innocently crying as she begged those pugnacious Muslims not to force their way into the house and take me away. She was not aware that I had begun my escape from Iran.

I ran as hard as I could, and my tears of fright were nearly blinding the path before me. While running I felt a sharp pain in my abdomen, but knew that I could not risk slowing my pace. I had to locate a pay phone to call Javid. I drew unwanted attention from other pedestrians as I sped past them. I was ter-rified that plain clothed policemen may have been watching the house. If someone told them about a running woman, they could easily find and arrest me. I got to a phone and called Javid's cell number, there was no answer. The Lord brought the number of Aman to my mind. He was the Turkish fellow who was to aid us in our journey. My hands were shaking as I told him what had happened. He instructed me to stop running and to calmly begin walking toward the nearest bus station. I was to do nothing that would draw attention and he assured me that he would be able to locate me for a pickup. I was frustrated and distraught that I had not been able to contact my husband.

SAFE HOUSE

A car pulled up next to the bus station and the driver motioned for me to get in. I was at first hesitant to do so. I never had seen Aman before, and for all I knew the driver could have been a secret policeman. With a prayer in my heart I gathered the courage to climb into the car. As he pulled away from the curb I just sat there, I was too frightened and winded to say a word. I was greatly relieved when Aman introduced himself and shook my hand. I buried my face in his shoulder as he told me that he was taking me to a safe house. I would be staying there until Javid, Reza and Bita joined me for the trip. After a 45 minute drive we pulled in front of a tall high-rise apartment building. We took the elevator to the 17th floor and went into a comfortable apartment that he said would be a safe haven from the authorities.

It was a very hectic day. I sat on the couch and cried. I could do nothing but praise God when Aman told me that he had located Javid and the other couple and that they would join us that evening. I spent the evening thinking over the events of what would be my last day in Tehran. I was very grateful that we had been able to have a peaceful meal with my parents Friday evening. I was glad that I had spontaneously kissed Mother and Father affectionately the night before. Thoughts of Mother's beautiful face and eyes broke into my memory. Perhaps she sensed that the end was near. She attempted to hide her tears behind her hijab and dried them with a tissue. I could not fight back the sobs while I came to the realization that those kisses had been my farewell to them. I cried myself into a deep sleep. I awoke late in the evening with Javid's face smiling down at me and inquiring if I was OK. Reza and Bita joined us later that evening. We learned that the prosecutor also had summoned them for arrest.

Aman delivered groceries to the apartment for us. He admonished us all that we were not to set foot out of the apartment until he said that it was safe to leave Tehran. He set a map on the table and explained the details of our route of escape that would take place as soon as possible. There were several possible routes. One would take us through Baluchestan to Pakistan. Another would go through to Oman via the Persian Gulf and the other through Kurdistan, a city in the Kurdish tribal area of North West Iran, to Turkey. The easiest route was to go southwest to Bandar Abbas. We would mix with other passengers and travel by boat through the Persian Gulf and on to Oman. While he spoke, that route was cancelled from the possibilities. He received a telephone call and spoke to someone in a language that we did not understand. He then told us that Iranian forces were alerted in the Persian Gulf for a possible attack by the Iraqis. It would be unwise of us to venture down that path.

CHOSEN PATH OF LIGHT

He told us that we would fly to Tabriz then drive to Kurdistan and from there we would have to go through the deserts and mountains into Ankara, Turkey. I was desperately concerned about my parents worrying about the possibility that the police had captured me. We spent our time praying together and reading the Bible for comfort and an undetected journey. Two days later Aman delivered our tickets for a 5:00 a.m. air flight to Tabriz, Iran the next day. From there his friends would help us to escape through the mountains to Ankara. This flight did not require passports, but we would have to show our ID cards for it. This would have to be covered with prayer. Our names were on the national black list, and if the authorities checked our names against the wanted list, we would be arrested. God would have to blind their eyes. Aman warned us that if we were caught, we would all be executed without a formal trial. He assigned us false names that we were to memorize. We were not to use our true names, even in speaking with one another, until we were safely out of the country. We were to use only these names if the heavily armed guards at the airport or the border crossings questioned us. He told us to expect that our car would be searched at different checkpoints between the border of Iran and Turkey. Our sole mission was survival.

Aman was our calm in the mist of the storm. He was accustomed to taking risks. Reza and Bita were excited, but visibly apprehensive. Javid and I were concerned for the life of the baby in my womb. I sat on the floor and Bita asked about how I was feeling. I simply could not talk. We all decided that timidity was not an option. We took faith in the mighty name of Jesus. The mention of that matchless name gave us a sense of courage that victory would come. Aman picked us up at 4:30 a.m. for our Monday morning flight on the last full day that we would spend in our home country. We each carried small pieces of hand luggage that contained a few clothes, toiletries and a little food for the journey.

DIPLOMATIC SERVICE

I rolled down the car window on the way to the airport. I wanted to feel Tehran's cool morning breeze on my face just one more time. To avoid detection we entered the airport by the back road and went through a separate entrance from the other passengers. It was very crowded and I felt woozy with fear and morning sickness. I could hardly walk and leaned on Javid for support. I nearly fainted when an airport customs officer approached Aman. He shook his hand and told us that he was one of his connections who would see to it that we got through all of the checkpoints for the flight. Aman hugged us goodbye and left us in the hands of the official. Without saying a word, he led us out the back exit of the airport and placed us in an airport car and drove us out to the plane. God was allowing us to receive diplomatic privileges. We did not even need boarding cards. The man saw to it that we were seated comfortably and disappeared from sight. Sorrowful questions flooded through my mind. Where was pastor Soodmand? Was he dead or alive? How much torture was Ali suffering in Evin prison? What were my poor parents thinking about my disappearance? Were they searching through the wicked Islamic system to locate me as they had Monir only several weeks previously? My seat by the window afforded me a last look at my beloved Tehran as we ascended into our destiny. My fellow escapees and I had committed our lives to the Lord for His safe keeping for this life and eternity. Our faith spoke that He would deliver us into a fresh life in an unknown land.

In the next chapter I will refrain from describing the exact route that we traveled though the remainder of our escape. To do so could endanger the lives of those who are still in the process of fleeing the horrors of Islam in Iran.

Chapter 4

THE PERILOUS JOURNEY TO FREEDOM

RESTAURANT CONFLICTS

That first day of travel had been exhausting and we were to meet Aman's contact at a certain hotel at 8:00 p.m. Shortly after we arrived in Tabriz, we approached the guesthouse and initiated the check-in process. Javid abruptly stopped his sign-in procedure and signaled for us to follow him outside. Anyone who is unfamiliar with Islamic regulations would assume that his gesture was needless. It was nothing of the kind. First there was the problem of our ID cards and our marriage contracts. It was mandatory that all persons checking into hotels show their ID cards. Couples who wanted to share a room had to show their marriage contracts. We could not show either, as it would reveal our true identities. Secret police were everywhere and the hotel attendants were obligated to call them if anyone looked suspicious. If we had gone through with registering at the hotel we would have been subjected to the very imprisonment that we were in the process of trying to avoid. We discussed the matter in the parking lot and even this drew suspicious glances from the hotel receptionist. Bita and I could have been arrested on charges of prostitution for standing in a public place at night. Javid saw this and directed us to the hotel's restaurant for further discussions. Things that are simple in America become incredibly complicated in Islamic cultures.

The restaurant was the scene of our first pressures with our traveling companions. Reza reasoned that it would be far easier if we went on separately because we drew suspicion traveling together. I took exception to the unstated implications of his opinion. I said, "Bita is your wife and I understand that you need to protect her. If you want to go on ahead of us you are welcome to do so. I know that it is a burden to travel with a sick pregnant woman."

Bita grabbed my hand and told him that our separation was out of the question. He apologized profusely and said that what he meant to say was that he and Javid could sleep in the streets while we stayed in the hotel. It was unreasonable concerning the circumstances, but I mentally compared the prospects of the hotel room to my own room at home. I deeply preferred the latter. Javid noticed my agitated expression and unsuccessfully attempted to console me. I was normally an easygoing person. This was an indication that the peculiarities of pregnancy were influencing me. The others realized my state and discussed things among themselves and notified me of their decisions.

We could not stay in the restaurant any longer without feeling that we had outstayed our welcome there. When we came out, the receptionist for the hotel was motioning for us to come and speak with him. Javid came back with a praise report. The receptionist had received a call from a friend of Aman's that liberated him to give us a single room without the necessity of registering at the front desk. Our agent of mercy then got into his car and left work for the evening. Javid and Reza went to the market to buy us some food, and Bita and I went to the room. The room was sparsely appointed with two single beds, a tiny table and two chairs. I buried my head in the pillow and hoped that Bita would not hear me weeping. I could not bear any more thoughts of covert wanderings through unknown territories.

The food that they brought was just as Aman had depicted that it might be: that of the native people. Just as my pregnant sisters before me, I was suffering from ongoing complications in my pregnancy. Any food would have been unappealing. The foods that the guys brought to the room were especially unattractive. I felt helpless. My only shelter was my faith in Christ.

Three hours later, Javid awakened me from my nap and insisted that I eat some fresh fruit. I wanted them to join me, and they declined as they wanted to make sure that the baby and I were getting enough nutrition. Their kindness did nothing but intensify my self-conscious awareness that I was a burden to everyone. Bita and I slept in the single beds, and Reza and Javid bedded down on the floor. I was grateful that I had a bed to sleep in before continuing our arduous journey through the deserts and then into the mountains. Before retiring for the night, we spent a great deal of time reading our Bibles and interceding about our excursion the next day. We alternated in voicing our prayers to Jesus.

A DRIVE IN SILENCE

I awoke at 9:00 a.m. and saw Javid having his morning devotions. Reza was out running errands pertinent to our departure at 8:00 that night. While Bita and I were still asleep, Javid had gone out and purchased our breakfast of fresh bread. Much to my chagrin, I could not eat due to my customary morning sickness. Drinking water was an equal trial. It was unwise for us to leave the room for two reasons: We had no false ID cards, and the army was on alert. Anyone without proper identification would be taken into the police station. Throughout the day we occupied our time with prayer and discussion, and wondered who our contact would be that night. Aman had told us that one of his contacts would come to our room and divulge our future traveling plans.

There was a knock at our door around 8:20 that night. A man entered who introduced himself as Mahmood, the friend of Aman. He came bearing food supplies for our journey. A car and driver waited for us in the hotel parking lot. We were to be driven to Kurdistan, which is near the border between Iran and

Turkey. The plan was that we were to stay in one of the native people's safe houses until it was safe to cross the border. When we climbed into the car, the driver did not utter a word as we greeted him. Mahmood took the front passenger seat and we crammed ourselves into the back seat. The whole ordeal made my heart pound and was very uncomfortable. Javid gave me a smile of assurance that all would go well.

Our attempts to enter discussions with Mahmood and the driver were futile. They seemed worried and were preoccupied with looking out for the authorities' checkpoints. We were empathically warned that if we were stopped we were not to look directly into the eyes of those questioning us.

None of us felt like talking, so we remained silent throughout the long drive. Mahmood noticed that I looked ill. Javid asked if we could rest for a while and our contact man barked that it would be impossible to stop. He questioned Javid about my ability to make the trip. Javid tried to get me to get some sleep. Sleep eluded me, because I was cold and sick and my nerves were frayed.

Again the question was asked, "Are you sure that your wife can handle the rough terrain that we have to take?" Javid told him that none of us could make it without the grace of God intervening for us. The roads became rougher and I frequently looked at my watch wondering when we would arrive at our first stopover point. After what seemed to be an eternity, the car stopped in front of a huge old house and Mahmood announced that we had arrived. We had no idea of the name of our first stopover village.

I'M ONE OF YOU

Our knock brought the response, "I'm coming, I'm coming. Stop knocking the neighbors might hear you." An older native woman opened the door, looked both ways, and then motioned for us all to enter as quickly as possible. Once we were inside she warmly greeted Bita and me with a kiss and seated us comfortably. The house was filled with the luscious scent of freshly baked bread. She scurried off and reentered with a tray of bread, cookies and tea. She discerned that I was with child and went back into the kitchen to prepare eggs and fresh yogurt for us. We did not know whether or not it was safe to speak of our escape in her presence. The group was relieved to learn that she was a specialist at smuggling people out of the country and that we could speak freely. Mahmood informed us that she would be assisting us for the first several hours when our journey resumed. He said that her age was an asset, as the guards did not suspect that someone of her advanced years would be involved with secret missions. We all became aware that the peaceful presence of the Almighty resided in her home. It was wonderful to relax in that atmosphere. The house was simple in its furnishings and we sat on the floor as we ate. She shared the meal with us and smilingly instructed me to eat well for the good of my baby. I was ravenous and gladly complied.

She provided us with comfortable blankets and sent us upstairs for the night. Mahmood again gave us a run-through of how we were to conduct ourselves: "Don't use your real names anywhere near the border and never look directly into the eyes of the authorities." He also gave us the plan for the continuation of our travel. He then slipped out for several hours to make the arrangements for us. As he was leaving I heard him instruct the kind old woman to take good care of us because we were special friends of his brother. I wondered just whose brother he was. He might have been a relative of Aman's because they had similar facial characteristics. The fresh breeze that came in through our bedroom door refreshed us as we talked before slipping off into deep slumbers on our mattresses.

Our hostess awakened us and, like a mother hen, told us to wash our faces. We sought the outhouse toilet and washed in the cool waters of the artesian well's pump. She then served us a marvelous Iranian country breakfast. Afterward she giggled at my attempt to help her wash the dishes. I think she might have guessed that I was from a wealthy family and likely doubted that I had ever washed a dish in my life. Nonetheless, I did a good job and put them in a plastic container to dry in the sun. Her home had no running water and she volunteered that in the winter she had to boil water to wash her dishes. It was enjoyable to spend the day observing the farm animals of rural Iran. She had a huge yard dog that frequently barked. It was our assumption that it served as a guard dog.

We stayed in the safe house for 5 days waiting for Mahmood's signal that we could launch our trek to the border. He was checking to see to it that the border guards who were suspicious of him would be off duty before we attempted a crossing. During our stay, our hostess became my dear friend in the Lord. The second night, I saw her reading her Bible and bowing her head in prayer. She noticed that I was watching her and motioned me over to come and sit with her. She smiled as she answered my unasked question. "Yes, I am one of you. I believe that Jesus is the Savior of the world and He lives in my heart. I came to know Him 11 years ago. She slipped to the floor and her eyes brimmed with tears and she began to tell me of her life. She pointed to a photograph on the wall of her only son. Six months previously, the Iraqi soldiers had killed him. She now lived a secluded life unless escapees came to her for safe haven. Her smile beamed through her tears as she spoke that she was not lonely because God's nearness could always be felt.

She asked if I really wanted to leave my country and why I had chosen to do so while in the midst of a pregnancy. I told her the whole story, which explained that I had not had any choice in the matter. She fully understood that our only choices were prison, torture and death or risking our lives though flight from our homes and nation. She had devoted her life to helping persecuted Christians. Upon hearing of our coming she had begun to pray for all that pertained to our escape. It was such a relief to be able to express myself freely, that I fell into her sweet, ancient arms and wept. She caressed my hair and gently reminded me that I could tell her anything, but that I must remember to be cautious in my speech around others on the journey. She said that even the tribal folks could be covert informants who would gladly accept the alleged rewards from Allah that could be derived in paradise for helping punish apostates like us.

TRIBAL ATTIRE

The fifth night, our elderly helper came upstairs and told us that our journey would resume early the next morning. She would deliver us to the pick-up site where Mahmood would rejoin us at 4:00 a.m. She provided us with tribal costumes to disguise our identities. She never ceased to demonstrate care for my unborn child and she packed peanuts, walnuts and raisins for me and the others to munch on along the way. She insisted that we go to sleep early so that we would be well rested for the trip. I struggled between faith and doubt about everything. I guessed that Bita was having similar troubles. Javid and Reza were our strong examples of Christian courage. The next morning we awoke to her soft voice calling to us, "Children it's time."

We all put on our local garb, and our senior citizen helper showed Bita and me how to adjust our veils into the style in which the women of that area wore them. She led us in prayer and we thanked her for her hospitality. We blessed her home and departed from her property for the first time in five days. Reza and Javid were instructed to walk ahead while she walked with Bita and me. Whenever there was a need to make a change in directions she would whisper the course to the men who were walking in front of us. After stumbling through the darkness for a while, we came upon a parked car.

The driver's three-year-old boy was sitting in the back seat. We were informed that he would help fool the officials about our intentions. Bita was instructed to hold him in her lap as though he was her own child. We drove for a few miles and the driver suddenly shouted, "You women get down out of sight!" I shook like a leaf in a storm as I crouched in the floor of the back seat. We were passing a checkpoint and had we looked suspicious, the guards would have stopped us and searched the car. Within a few moments he gave us the OK and we resumed our seats. I was silently praying to regain my composure, and several hours later the alarm went off again.

BROKEN RULES

The traffic had come to a halt, and the driver had gone to see why there was a holdup. He reported that the security forces had blocked the road ahead and were examining everyone's papers. We wanted to turn around, but there was no way that we could do so without looking conspicuous. About 30 minutes later two officials were peering into the car with their guns drawn. My back ached with pain and I was almost dying of fright. I called upon the Lord to help me keep from drawing attention to myself. Surely the others were going through the same process. The boy was asleep in Bita's lap and she was nestling her face against his. I broke the rules by momentarily looking into the guard's face as he studied each of us.

"Where are you going?" Our driver named the village. "What is your business there?"

"My sister is in labor and our women are going to serve as midwives in her child's birth." The guy sighed impatiently and commanded us to move on. Reza blessed the Lord for all of us, and I finally took a breath that was not constricted by fearful tension. The driver stared at my reflection in his rearview mirror and began to scold me, "Why did you look into his eyes? You know better than that. Don't dare do it again." I meekly apologized to the group.

THE ARMY JEEP

Several hours later the mountains came into view. Had the circumstances been different, it would have been a pleasant drive. We passed through a tunnel and parked near what appeared to be a cave on the other side of the mountain. An army jeep was parked there, and its driver signaled for us to follow him. Surprisingly, our driver did so without hesitation. The helpful old smuggler told us that it was now time for us to separate. I would deeply miss her. She had held my hand for the entire journey up to that juncture. I expressed that I wished that she would come with us. She smiled and told us that we were in good hands and said that we would soon be meeting up with Mahmood again. She hugged us goodbye and we boarded the jeep with our few belongings. Our old companion's parting words to me were that I was to eat plenty of nutritious foods for my baby's welfare. She was blessing us in the name of Jesus as her car pulled away. The new driver asked for all of our identification documents and explained that, if we were caught, it would be best that we did not have them in our possession. We gave him our precious marriage contracts and official identity cards. He assured us that they would be returned to us when we reached Ankara, Turkey.

The heat caused us to keep the windows down even though it was incredibly dusty. The thing that we traveled upon could not qualify as a road. It was more of a goat path. The jeep was far from comfortable. But it was the best mode of transportation in that terrain, and army jeeps did not draw unwanted attention. We all praised God when we were switched into another real car. We were past the roughest areas and we quickly transferred our things into the waiting car. The car's driver commented that it was good that we were covered with dust. For the sake of curious security personnel, it made us appear more like humble tribal people rather than sophisticates. The road was strewn with stones and bumpy as we drove further into the steep mountains.

Suddenly we heard gunshots. Armed officials who were posted on the mountaintop were aiming their weapons right at us. My young mind lunged into despair and I held my head in my hands. I inwardly mused that it would have been better to die in Evin prison than in this forsaken place. Our guide quickly demanded that if questioned we were to say nothing. He would do all of the talking for us. The driver exited the car and raised his hands in surrender. Within the car, we followed suit as the guards approached. We all chanted, "In Jesus' name, in Jesus' name," under our breaths.

"What are you doing in this area? Show me your identity card. Where are you going?"

"We are taking our wives to help my sister. She is in labor and about to give birth to a set of twins."

"Where are the identify cards of the others?"

At this point our driver demonstrated that he was clever and experienced. He angrily shouted, "What kind of Muslim do you think that I am? I would never show my wife's face to a stranger."

The man responded in shock, "You are insane. Get out of here and don't let me see you again." He motioned to those on the mountaintop who still had their guns trained on us to let us pass. We sped away, and the driver laughed gleefully, but Bita and I were still quite shaken by the experience.

NOT SO FAST

Our driver drove like he really was insane. None of us understood how he could keep the car on the road as it flew around the curves. It was obvious that he knew every inch of the territory. After a full day of his racecar antics, we were all grateful when he pulled into a village guesthouse. The driver said that he would depart and that Mahmood would be taking us the rest of the way in the morning. Darkness had closed in on us and we felt strangely alone when we heard that he was leaving us. He reported that there was only one room left in the inn. He instructed us to go in without knocking and to wait Mahmood's arrival. Javid pleaded with him not to leave us and to stay the night with us. We did not want to be strangers alone in that tribal area. He insisted that he would sleep in the car until our friend relieved his watch over us.

The room had the least furniture of anywhere that we had stayed. There was a jug of water for drinking and washing. Two dirty, well-worn rugs covered the floor, and a rickety oil-burning stove sat in the corner with a small box of matches beside it. Pieces of wood were strewn on the floor and pillows for us to sleep upon were propped against one of the walls. It was quite a comedown for rich kids. The driver told us to light the burner to give us light. We were all exhausted and none of us complained when we discovered that the water supply was inadequate for our personal hygiene needs. We ladies splashed a little water on our faces and wiped the dust away with our hijabs.

Of course, I could not go to sleep without browbeating myself for the fear I had exhibited during the day. The fact that my feet were swollen, my back ached, and that I felt uncomfortably bloated did not help my emotional state. I dozed off for a moment and snapped to when I heard Mahmood's voice. He relieved the other driver and then presented us with the food that he had brought for us. I was dead tired and wanted to lie down. However, it would have been culturally impolite to do so in the presence of an older person who was a guest in our room. Mahmood inquired about our days of separation and I said, "Scary!"

He chuckled, "Wait for the remainder of the trip. It has been a picnic up until now compared to what you will soon experience. You will find out what scary really means." We tried to convince him to sleep in the room. He walked out explaining that he preferred the moonlit mountains for his blanket as he kept watch over us. Finally a sound sleep overtook us all. Our schedule demanded that it end before sunrise.

MAHMOOD REAPPEARS

The wee hours of the morning inevitably broke in upon us and we all arose from our slumbers. As usual, Mahmood's voice was our alarm clock. I had trouble opening my eyes, and when I did mange to peek through them I found that I had a terrible headache. Then it dawned on me that it was time to resume our travels. I wanted my nice home in Tehran. I wanted to be with my parents for the birth of their grandchild. And if I had any tears left, I just wanted to shed them. Regret for all that had occurred momentarily beamed into my mind. Perhaps I had been silly to give up a life that most Muslim and Christian girls never experience in their lifetimes. Perhaps I had been foolish to trade my education and bright future for a new religion. Within seconds the Holy Spirit reminded me of the harsh realities of Islam that I had been saved from. Instantly, I knew that I could never regret my belief in Christ. At times the joy of the Holy Spirit filled my mind to the extent that I felt as though I was in heaven. Occasionally, while we traveled through the mountains, the good thoughts were momentarily blurred and it seemed that I was adrift in the ocean of despair. We made our morning tea on the stove and ate the breakfast of bread and cheese that had arrived with our guide. Our things were loaded into the vehicle and off we went into the darkness of the morning.

To the glory of God we drove the entire day without encountering any hostile forces. It was 11:15 p.m. when I checked my watch. Our bodies yearned for rest from road jar. Mahmood said that it would be less than prudent to stop. The men that could instantly end our lives would be covering the countryside like ants during daylight hours. Intermittently, he refueled the jeep from the cans that were strapped to its back bumper. When he did so, the others satisfied their hunger with the leftovers from breakfast. I offered Bita some of my nuts and raisins, but she declined in deference to my condition. At 3:30 a.m. I told the group that within 30 minutes we would have been on the road for 24 straight hours. During that time, my feet and back continued to throb. The cramped conditions forbade me from finding relief by shifting my body around. Periodically I would lay my head on Bita's lap. Just as I was about to yell that I could not bear another inch of the road, it was announced that we would be resting for the entire day. With that, the driver pulled in front of another village dwelling. I felt like shouting praises.

ANOTHER KIND VILLAGER

Its owner welcomed us and introduced us to his family. After the formalities, we began to wash the millions of dust particles from our faces. I felt the grains of dust in my mouth every time my teeth met. I soaked my swollen feet in warm water that our hostess had prepared for me. We ate her stew. My head swam with dizziness, but the pains in my back minimized the effect of my dizziness. Bita administered vitamins to me. Javid did all in his power to make me comfortable. Mahmood announced that he would be back later, and disappeared. My exhaustion enabled me to out sleep the others. The nights tended to be bitter cold in the mountains, making the extra blankets that we carried a blessing. I did not awaken until late in the day. Mahmood reappeared when night fell. For the next 72 hours our schedule remained the same. We would drive from sunset till dawn and then rest out of the sight of the authorities during the day. Our driver and guide never ceased to amaze us with his nighttime maneuvering skills. Unquestionably he had made this trek so many times that he knew the path by heart.

The schedule significantly changed on the fourth night. Mahmood said that we should not continue further, and that we would have to camp out in the mountains. He did not give a reason for the change and that was worrisome. It was windy and the night air was frigid when we got out of the jeep. A fire was built and everyone prepared the blankets for a night on the ground. Javid tried to give me his blanket and I refused it. I could not bear the thought of him freezing during the night.

Our guide was questioned about when we would begin again and his answer was that he was not sure. None of us welcomed the prospects of camping out in the mountains for an extended period of time. The others were sitting around the fire talking when I fell asleep with my head in Javid's lap. My body ached from the discomfort of the hard ground beneath me. When I heard the word that it was time to go, I found that Javid had disregarded my request and put his blanket over me. I asked if it was safe to begin travel again and Mahmood's only response was that he hoped so. We drove for only a short while and stopped where there was a man who seemed to be waiting for us. He held the reins of a pair of donkeys.

THE RUDE DONKEY GUY

Mahmood directed that each couple was to mount one of the animals and that we were to follow the villager until we came to the spot where another car would meet us. Mahmood performed another one of his disappearing acts and drove off into the darkness. To this day I do not know how he ever got any rest and what it is exactly he was doing during the hours that he was separated from us. Javid preferred to walk with our new guide and we tailed behind them. After about two hours the man sullenly told us to dismount. We did so and tethered the beasts to some trees. We just blankly stared at him awaiting further instructions. In an irritated manner he asked what we were staring at, then commanded, "Follow me."

Bita asked if he was implying that we were to walk behind him.

"No, you should fly," he answered sarcastically. "Of course you have to walk because we all must go by foot for the next stage of the journey."

Javid complained on my behalf that I had swollen feet and that it would be impossible for me to walk. The guide yelled at him. No one that we had encountered had treated us in such a rude manner.

"Your wife's swollen feet are not my problem. You will all follow me on foot until I say that it is OK to stop."

I leaned upon Javid and walked as best as I could. The pain in my feet and back were sapping my energies. It was difficult to bear walking for long periods. During one of our momentary rest stops, I examined my feet and discovered that one of my big toes was bleeding. My shoe was filled with blood. I secretly wiped away the blood and made a makeshift bandage for it without telling the others my condition. I was determined to finish the course without being a further burden on the group. I don't think that anyone has the answers for why those who accept Jesus often experience such pains.

THE LOST TREASURE

I saw the sun peeking over the mountains behind us and looked down to check the time. The treasured diamond-studded wristwatch that my mother had given me for my birthday one year before was gone. The emotions that flooded through me because of this loss, coupled with my physical pain, made me grimace even more as I walked. The man noticed and offered his first kind words: "We will be meeting a car in about 20 minutes." Bita told us that it was around 8:00 a.m.

We rounded a bend and were shocked to see the Iranian flag flying over a shack. Armed military personnel were everywhere and a sign on the shack said, "Stop – Checkpoint." Our guide whispered that this would be one of the most dangerous parts of our trip. We circled around the checkpoint and the wind and dust blew against us. After we had crossed over behind it we hid in the cover of some large bushes. Our guide said that we were to stay low and to keep moving. We all understood that even though the Lord had helped us pass the checkpoint, we were still within range of their rifles if they spotted us. Then, a most appreciated sight came into view. Mahmood was standing next to a car smiling at us. Before bidding us goodbye, the guide apologized for yelling at us. He said that he had treated us roughly just to keep us moving on schedule. While we pulled away, Mahmood confided that we had another military check station coming up. At the beginning of our travels with him, he warned that there were two types of inspectors that we could encounter along the way. One group was the soldiers. They were not that difficult to fool because most of them had been drafted and really preferred to be at home rather than checking people's documents. The other group was the official Islamic guards. Those guys made a career of catching people like us. They delighted in hassling ordinary people with ruthless displays of their authority. We all sighed in relief when Mahmood told us that soldiers manned the outpost ahead and that one of them was his friend.

HELPFUL FRIENDS

One of the soldiers greeted Mahmood with a hug and peeked into the car window asking who we were. We were identified as family members that he was taking on a brief outing to the other side. The soldier warned that the area was crawling with official Islamic guards. To prevent us from being hassled by them he took us to an old villager's quaint home. We waited out the remainder of the day there. The elderly man lived alone and I think he may have been happy to have our company. We refreshed ourselves with the simple foods that he offered and slept for several hours.

Mahmood led us out into the night wind that became a full-blown sandstorm. We were again on foot. The night was so black that our husbands had to take our hands to guide us. Had our guide not been so skillful, we could have easily lost our way in the dust, wind and freezing temperatures. The sand beat against our bodies and stung our eyes. If Mahmood had not goaded us into marching on we would have easily sought refuge from that storm. He interpreted it as a blessing in disguise because it would prevent the Islamic guards from venturing out. We walked through the night under the most difficult circumstances that we had run into during our trek to freedom. At daylight the storm blew itself out and the weather become warmer. This time not only my feet ached, everyone's were bruised and also aching. It was God who got us through that night and kept us from being discovered during the day. The sandy dust that clung to our clothing made us appear as ghosts as we approached a man holding three horses in a valley that ran between two mountains.

RIDING DOUBLE

Mahmood returned all of our identification documents to us. We mounted the horses and trotted behind him. All I could do was hang on to Javid with my eyes closed as our mount rapidly took the hills and valleys. The going got rougher and

Mahmood dismounted and led his horse around a steep ravine. We wanted to do the same, but he demanded that we stay saddled. We came to a halt when a man came up to him and hugged him. He had been standing by a car with a group of men. The fellow smiled and said, "Turkey! Turkey!"

We looked at him in disbelief and Mahmood pointed westward and gave us the blessed news. "That my friends, is Turkey." He then told us that we would be separating for the final time. When we bade our champion a final goodbye, Bita and I would have liked to hug him like our husbands did. Propriety demanded that we only shake his hand. Javid called him a great man and promised that he would always be in his prayers as he hugged him for the last time. Mahmood parted by blessing us in the name of the Lord. He said that he hoped to meet us agin when we would be entering rather than exiting Iranian soil. I wept because I had passed from the Kurdish tribal area of Iran and now stood on the brink of never setting foot on Iranian soil again.

DINGY DUMP

The Turkish man hurried us into the jeep. I looked out the rear window and saw faithful Mahmood and the horses disappearing in a cloud of dust. After traveling for a little way, we asked if we were in Iran or Turkey. "You are on the outskirts of Ankara, Turkey." I smiled as Javid hugged me. I knew that we were in Turkey when the road beneath us became asphalt rather than dirt. I also noted the women's distinctive head coverings that were different in style from those that we wore. We all gave thanks to the Lord that He had delivered us from the many dangers that we had faced in Iran. The dangers were not over, however. Turkey was also in the grip of Islam. The Turks did not trust the Iranians and many of them were radical Muslims who would have liked nothing better than to turn us over to the authorities.

It took us almost two weeks to make the journey into Turkey. We were all exhausted, but nonetheless were praising

God that we had reached Ankara safely. After four hours of dri-
ving around, our driver deposited us with one of Aman's
contacts whose name was Abi. He spoke fluent Arabic, but we
could not identify the Middle Eastern country of his origin. He
had been assigned the responsibility of securing lodging for us.
Because of Aman's good reputation with us, we assumed that
this fellow would house us in a decent abode. We were sadly
mistaken. It turned out that his attitude was duplicated within
many of the middlemen that were supposed to help us in
Turkey. It made little difference to him that none of us had
showered in two weeks and that my body was wracked with
pain. He was rude, un-talkative, and acted as though he was
very suspicious of us. He dumped us at the most filthy place
that I had ever seen. He insisted that it was the best place for us
because we were short on funds and barely had sufficient
money to even feed ourselves. Most of the money I had taken
from my father's cash drawer had gone to buy food and pay the
smugglers. There was a fellow sitting at the front desk with 50
passports scattered before him. He was sealing them in
envelopes. It appeared that he had a part-time business of
making false passports. The other occupants of the building
looked like homeless drug addicts and fugitives from justice.
The building itself was actually in ruins and rodents, roaches
and ants crawled everywhere. We bought a little tea and some
bread and cheese and went to our horrid room. Abi was a
tremendous disappointment to us.

THE LETTER

I desperately wanted to get in contact with my parents. It was
probable that they were still under suspicion and that the phone
lines were still being tapped. Therefore, I decided that I would
write them a letter. It was my hope that concentrating on the
letter to them would distract my mind from my physical discom-
forts and also let them know that we were all right. I did not put a
return address on the envelope because I did not want Iran's
Islamic secret police to come and drag us back or to execute us

right there in Ankara. I understood that my parents would discern our general location from the Turkish postage stamp on the letter.

Dearest Father and Mother in the whole world,

I am writing to let you know that we are alive and well in a nearby country. It has been almost a month sine we last saw one another. Mother, I will never forget how horrible it was to see those tears flowing down your angelic cheeks and hear your screams coming from your lips when the authorities came to arrest me. Please forgive me for all of the troubles that I have put both of you through. I miss you so much that the paper of this letter is wet from my tears of sorrow. I will have to let it dry before I can mail it on to you.

Father, I know that you remember all the questions that I used to ask you about God and the Koran. I have found my answers in Christianity. It all started when I began reading the Bible that I had found in the library. It spoke to me in a manner that all of our Islamic rituals never had. The Lord Jesus revealed Himself to me as the truth, the life and the way in a spiritual dream one night. There is a verse in the Bible that says that very same thing about Him. Shortly after that I discovered that Monir was also a Christian and I began to attend meetings with her. I was gloriously converted to Christ and now I know that He lives in my heart. Four days before our marriage, I saw Javid at one of the secret Christian meetings. I had no idea that he had been converted shortly after returning from the Iraqi war. He too discovered that Jesus is far more than a prophet. He is the Savior of the world. Now that we are in a foreign nation, His personal presence continues to be our source of strength.

This letter is to let you know that we are alive in spirit as well as in the flesh. My pregnancy has caused a few health problems with swelling, bleeding feet and so forth, but I have the confidence that I will be all right. It is my prayer that I will see your beautiful faces again when I show you my wonderful first baby after its birth. I am respectfully kissing this paper as I would your hands if I was with you in person. Again, I beg you to forgive me. Please accept me for whom I now am, a child of the Living God who has Jesus, His Son, in her heart.

Your loving daughter,
Mina

REJECTION

I laid my hands on the letter and prayed for the Holy Spirit's anointing power to be upon it as my parents read it. I then slipped it into the postal box. The hardest blow of my life came two weeks after I had posted the letter. In an effort to make sure that they had received it, I risked everything and called their home. I was relieved that mother answered the phone. From the moment of my, "Hello, Mother," she initiated an interrogation. She wept as she said, "Why did you write that letter? How could you do that to us? The officials were censoring our mail and they called your father in for questioning. While they read him your letter, he suffered a heart attack and had to be hospitalized."

My mother's outburst put me in a state of shock. It intensified as my father grabbed the receiver from her, "Mina, listen very carefully to what I am going to say. Your conduct has brought great shame on this family. Since you foolishly sent that letter, the authorities now have your handwritten confession that you are a Kafar, an infidel Christian." By this time he was screaming over the phone. "It is now clear that you deceived us with many lies. From this point forward, you are not my daughter and I am rejecting you. I have no child named Mina. No one in this household will ever be allowed to mention your name or speak to you again. Do you understand? I have erased every memory of you from our home and identity cards. You no longer exist. You are an ingrate girl." With that, he hung up on me.

My father had been angry when I prayed in Farsi and even angrier when I brought home the Bible. This tirade eclipsed anything that I ever imagined could come from his lips. A wall of stone had been erected between my family, my nation and me. The price of my faith in Christ was that I could never return to Tehran unless there was a monumental change in its government. I fell by the telephone booth into a puddle of wailing tears. I drew unwanted attention from those who passed by. A Turk asked if I needed assistance and I declined by shaking my head. I was afraid that the police would arrest me right there on the street if I acted disorderly. This could mean that we would all be sent back to suffer our fates in Iran. Dizziness overcame me and I could hardly pull myself to my feet. I attempted to adjust my veil properly and to walk without crying. My father's voice echoed in my ears with every painful step that I took.

PAIN OF ALL PAINS

Somehow I made it to the dumpish guesthouse and headed up the stairs. I felt very dizzy and a piercing pain shot through my lower abdominal area. After taking several steps I fainted and toppled back down the stairs. I came to and saw Javid and a Turkish nurse standing there in our despicable room. Javid broke the heartrending news to me. The stress, the donkey and horseback rides, poor nourishment and little rest had taken their toll. I had miscarried our child. This catapulted me into a physical, emotional and spiritual downward spiral. My broken heart caused tears to flow profusely as the nurse held me in her arms. It was very difficult to reconcile our prayers for protection with the fact that the miscarriage had occurred after we had made it through the mountains and thought we were safe in Turkey. Javid was very upset about all that had transpired. If I were not already in such poor shape, Javid would have reprimanded me for calling my parents' home. He too was shocked that my father had disowned me.

I wanted to call my mother. Perhaps she could give me some hope that the entire family had not abandoned the knowledge that I had been a family member. She was a Muslim, but had never been as intense about it as my father and brothers. Religion could never hinder her love for her children. I gave her a call and by the Lord's grace she answered the phone. I told her about the baby and she wept for us both.

"My poor daughter. My poor little grandchild." She consoled me by confessing that she had never rejected me in her heart. She would always love me though she had to comply with my father's wishes that I be shunned. She said that after our previous phone call she had secretly given praise to Allah that I was alive. We said our goodbyes with expressions of love and ended the call. My spirits began to regain vitality after I had spoken with her. It was invigorating to learn that there was still one family member who loved and missed me.

CRUEL TALONS

Javid and I sensed that the cruel talons of Islam were poised to snare us there in Turkey. There are numerous things that Westerners simply do not have the capacity to understand about the Muslim world because their thinking is based upon Judeo-Christian perspectives. In the West an enemy of one's nation is one's enemy regardless of their religion. Under Islam, Muslims from opposing nationalities can slaughter one another over political issues. However, if a Muslim of one nationality forsakes Islam, those of the opposing Muslim nations would feel obligated to punish them as if the offender was a member of their own nationality. Islam is a dark religion that unifies nationalities in its barbarisms and religious persecutions. Therefore, as long as we remained in a Muslim country, at any moment we could undergo serious consequences and deportation if it was discovered that we were Muslims who had converted to Christianity. In other words, Turkish radicals were just as dangerous to us as Iranian radicals. We all realized that we had to find an avenue of escape from Turkey and the poisoned web of Islam. This understanding put us under an incessant sense of pressure.

UPS AND DOWNS

In addition to this, Javid and I were fighting our own emotional and spiritual battles. I cannot accurately depict what Javid was going through. He is a courageous man who values others above himself. He did not risk putting me into further discouragement by telling me how he really felt about all that had happened. On the emotional level, my sorrow about the loss of my baby increased as time progressed. It was like the shock of breaking a bone in one's leg. At first the body overrides the pain and numbness sets in. However, as soon as the body relaxes from its shocked mode, the pain becomes unbearable. That is the way my heart felt. It was as though someone had cut a lonely hole in my soul and never bothered to give it the attention that it needed. Of course, the rejection of my father added to this trauma. On the physical level, I was very ill because we did not have the resources to get the full medical treatments that I needed after the miscarriage. The pains were excruciating and it felt like my energy for life was oozing from my body.

Both Javid and I were undergoing another form of attack. Its source was someone whom mature Christians recognize as an adversary, Satan. It is his habit to present things that are evil as attractive and harmless and things that are good as unattractive and evil. He battered our souls with doubts at every opportunity in relation to Islam and Christianity. Islam was presented as benign and Christianity as problematic. He brought memories of the good things that we had experienced with our Muslim parents as we were growing up. The truth was that the good things that resided in our parent's personalities were present in spite of Islam, not because of it. Satan, of course, tried to blur our remembrances of the depths of the evils that he had spawned in the heart of Muhammad. For instance, in strict Islamic cultures it is forbidden for any man other than a woman's husband to look on her nakedness. If there are no female physicians available, women go without necessary gynecological exams. The Hadith records an incident wherein Muhammed instructed a woman about how to cut the clitorises from young girl's bodies (Sunan of Abu Dawud, Chapter 1888). This barbaric female genital mutilation procedure is still practiced in many Muslim societies. It is just as the Bible says; *the dark places of the earth are full of the habitations of cruelty* (Psa. 74:20).

The only thing that kept us going during the Satanic onslaughts was the "still small voice" of the Holy Spirit from within us. He let us know that though God had not orchestrated all that had happened to us, He was able to weave everything into the fabric of our lives in a manner that was best for our temporal good and His eternal glory. The voice of the Lord and the power of the Word of God helped us overcome Satanic, spiritual, emotional and physical obstacles. During times that I ran high fevers, Javid and our companions followed the injunctions of the scriptures. They laid hands on me and prayed in faith for my recovery. I have no doubts that I would have perished in that vermin-infested room had it not been for their prayers.

UNVEILED

In Ankara I made a monumental decision that turned out to be my final severance from the bondages of my past as a Muslim woman. I discarded my hijab in the liberty of the name of Jesus. My first thought about wearing my veil was that I would always do so and thus follow Monir's example. It was part of her cover that permitted her to distribute Christian materials throughout Iran. In addition, I had worn it since I was nine years old and wearing a veil during our trek through the mountains had proved fruitful as a disguise. At first I felt shyly conspicuous without it because I was so accustomed to adorning myself with it before going into public. This shyness was the evidence of religious bondage. It had nothing to do with my actual feelings of self-esteem as an educated, progressive member of the Body of Christ. My only regret about removing it was momentary. When I called my mother, she hung up on me when she learned that I no longer wore the hijab. Perhaps for her it was a disappointing sign that I was drifting further from being the daughter she knew and loved. I clearly recognized that if I remained compliant with her wishes, it would hinder my growth as a believer. It was like unwrapping chains of fear from my soul and body.

The battle to survive there in Turkey without sufficient resources was taxing on all of us. One of the things that made our days bearable was that we exchanged testimonies with Reza and Bita. Each couple found the others' as encouraging tributes to the grace of God and the power of salvation.

BITA'S STORY

One day Bita shared her testimony and asked that I record it in my diary. She was quite confident that I possessed my grandfather's knack for writing and that someday I would write a book about our adventures. An added benefit of our talking with one another about the triumphs of the Lord in our lives was that it transformed our tears of weeping into tears of joy in the Lord.

Bita had been orphaned in a tragic car accident that took both of her parents when she was only six years old. Her father had left her and her sister a sizable endowment. Her uncle, who took the girls into his home, squandered their funds on his own selfish pursuits. He moved his family into a house that had belonged to their father and the girls became servants for his family until Bita finally ran away at the age of seventeen. He was a typical Muslim who did not see the sense in girls becoming educated, and he forbade them to go to school. They both loved to read and educated themselves while he was away from the home each day. Newspapers served as both reading and writing materials for them. Their cruel uncle would often have drunken parties at the home. The girls suffered numerous beatings from him when he went into his drunken rages.

Bita bloomed into a beautiful young woman who had a regal bearing. One of the wealthy business partners at her uncle's place of employment wanted to wed her. Her uncle agreed without consulting Bita. When he informed her of the situation, saying that the contract was settled, she said that she did not want to marry the man. Her uncle did not want to risk public embarrassment and he slapped Bita so hard that she went deaf in her right ear. A couple of days later the man came to discuss the wedding and arrived before her uncle got home from attending to an emergency. She wanted to run from the house but she did not know where she could go. She knew that if she ran and her uncle found her that he might beat her to death. If she stayed she would be like one of the thousands of Muslim women who were trapped in terrible marriages with men whom they did not know, much less love.

As all of this was spinning through her brain the doorbell chimed and Hossein, her intended husband, was at the door. Upon hearing that there was no man in the house he forced his way in and sexually assaulted her. He exited the house leaving Bita huddled in a corner crying from shock and pain. When she was telling me this part of her story she was reliving the event and shook with fear. I asked her to stop because it was upsetting her. She insisted that it was important that I know the whole story. As I listened, my contempt for Islam was intensified. Many Islamic women's husbands and fathers subject them to all forms of barbarism and no one does anything about it. Though such things are commonly reported by international women's rights organizations, the diplomats of the West continue to proclaim that Islam is a noble religion. I wonder if they would shout complaints rather than politically correct jargon if there was no oil in the Middle East?

She told her uncles what Hossein had done to her. He went into a rage, accusing her of lying so that the wedding would be cancelled, and severely beat her. From that point on she moved about the house in depressed despair. Several months later she was found to be with child and her uncle realized that her report had been true about the rape. However, his financial investments were more precious to him than Bita, so he did not confront his business associate about the matter. Bita was sentenced to a quick marriage with cruel Hossein in an effort to avoid public embarrassment over her pregnancy. The Islamic authorities could have executed her for being with child out of wedlock.

Her life became even more of a hell on earth. She delivered a male child and was never allowed to be his primary parent. Her wicked mother-in-law hovered over the child and denied Bita any influence in his life. Her roguish husband beat her frequently and she developed significant health problems. The beatings severely crippled her right leg and she could not walk without the assistance of a cane. I wish I had adequate words to convey what she must have been feeling. It is terrible when a beautiful person becomes the whipping post and sexual toy of an insensitive husband who treats her like a medieval house slave. After five unbearable years she began to make plans to run away. This necessitated that she make the hard decision to leave her little son behind. She loved him deeply, but he hardly knew her as his mother and if she attempted to take him he might cry out and draw attention to her escape. She ran away in the darkness and sought refuge in the home of one of her childhood friends who happened to live in the same building as Ali. It was the same apartment building where the secret meetings were held.

JESUS THE HEALER

Bita grew weary of the pain in her leg and hobbling around with her cane. She began to beg Allah to heal her though there is no history of miraculous healings in Islam. Then a life-changing event occurred. Ali came to her friend's apartment to borrow a screwdriver. Bita answered the door and Ali saw that she was in pain. After introducing himself, he spontaneously prayed for her leg to be healed. He then left the apartment and soon returned with a Farsi Bible for her. He departed with the screwdriver and she noticed that her leg felt better and that a peace that she had never known had come over her. Shortly afterward Ali, his wife and Monir prayed about inviting Bita to their Christian home group. They all had the witness that it was OK to invite her. Bita and Monir developed a close relationship. The group prayed for her to be healed, and that night she boldly confessed that Jesus was her Savior and Lord.

She went out for a walk after the meeting and slipped and fell. Her cane landed some distance from her. Her mind was filled with the thought that she had to get to her cane. It came to her memory that the Bible that she had been reading said that Jesus healed the lame. "Jesus, help me. Help me to stand up. I know that You are my healer." At first she could hardly get up and she prayed for a second time. She began to make struggling steps toward her cane and repeatedly said, "In Jesus' name." To her amazement she discovered that the power of God had rendered her every whit whole. She shouted praises to the living God into the darkness in thanksgiving for her healing. She cast the cane aside and never picked it up again.

From that point forward she never ceased giving praise to the Lord and was subsequently filled with the Holy Spirit. As she told me about her miraculous healing that night she lifted her hands heavenward and worshipped her King. I huddled in amazement in the corner of the dingy room and sensed the glory of God as she repeated over and over, "Amen, hallelujah." She then continued her story by relating how she had met her beloved Reza and how he had come to know the Lord. Hearing her talk temporarily relieved my worries about the perils of our situation. I could feel a renewal by the Spirit moving through my soul and body.

I attempted to get through to my mother again and my father answered the phone. He repeated his position in a very serious tone and I sadly hung up the phone. My emotions took drastic sways from one day to the next. In part, I attribute this to my physical condition that was brought on by the miscarriage. We had no money for medical care and fevers from the infection in my body often plagued me. At times I would rejoice in the Lord and could feel His peace. At other times the enemy would lead me down the dark path of questioning why I had converted to Christianity. Had my dear Monir been martyred in vain? The shame that my father's personal documents were now stamped with the insignia that let all know that he had an apostate daughter was a real burden to me. I had to fight cultivating a rabid hatred for those who had robbed me of my family, murdered my friend and imprisoned Ali. As a believer, my only choice was to forgive them as Christ had forgiven me. The prayers of the group and the power of God's Word snapped me out of Satan's doldrums whenever they befell me.

COMFORT IN JOB

The story of Job's faith in the midst of his trials was a source of comfort to me. Job 1:13-21 - *Now there was a day when his sons and daughters were eating and drinking wine in their oldest brother's house; [14] and a messenger came to Job and said, "The oxen were plowing and the donkeys feeding beside them, [15] when the Sabeans raided them and took them away—indeed they have killed the servants with the edge of the sword; and I alone have escaped to tell you!" [16] While he was still speaking, another also came and said, "The fire of God fell from heaven and burned up the sheep and the servants, and consumed them; and I alone have escaped to tell you!" [17] While he was still speaking, another also came and said, "The Chaldeans formed three bands, raided the camels and took them away, yes, and killed the servants with the edge of the sword; and I alone have escaped to tell you!" [18] While he was still speaking, another also came and said, "Your sons and daughters were eating and drinking wine in their oldest brother's house, [19] and suddenly a great wind came from across the wilderness and struck the four corners of the house, and it fell on the young people, and they are dead; and I alone have escaped to tell you!" [20] Then Job arose, tore his robe, and shaved his head; and he fell to the ground and worshiped. [21] And he said:*

"Naked I came from my mother's womb, And naked shall I return there. The Lord gave, and the Lord has taken away; Blessed be the name of the Lord."

Our stay in Ankara lasted seven weeks. The lessons we learned there have lasted us until this day. It was there that I cultivated a lively devotional life that gives me the assurance of God's presence every time that I come before His throne of grace. Most importantly, I learned not to be swayed by my emotions. They are at best unreliable and are often subjected to the devil's condemning accusations. We all began to concentrate on getting out of Turkey and into a nation that was not under the shadow of Islam. It would be such a blessing to live in a country where we could worship the Lord and witness freely of His grace. Things began to move in our favor when we began to pray with fasting for God's deliverance.

UP, UP AND AWAY

An Ankara news broadcast had announced that Iran and Turkey had made a pact. They would unite in a cooperative effort to deport any Iranian that was in Turkey without a proper visa back to Iran. A few days later I awoke to find that I was alone in the room. Bita left a note explaining that she and the guys were out running errands. This worried me and I wondered where they went and when they would return. Bita was back by early afternoon but the men had not returned. I inquired about the nature of their errands. Bita left again without giving me any clear explanation. I was uncomfortable about leaving the room and I did not enjoy staying alone without knowing what might be happening to them while out of my sight. Evening fell and they had not come back. My mind flooded over with concern for their safety. What if the authorities had checked their papers and found that they were illegal Iranian aliens? They would be deported and I would be left alone without knowing what had become of them.

Reza was the first to appear late in the evening and the others trailed in behind him. I was irate and they all were gleeful. Javid hugged me and announced that they had found a contact that could get us safely to Spain and then to a more secure country. The man met us that evening and explained that the journey would be risky, but not impossible. He had contacts in the various official agencies of the police and airport authorities that would overlook our lack of proper documents. We were to depart the country from the airport on the following Wednesday. The next five days seemed like 500 years.

We were to meet him in the airport and he showed up about 30 minutes late. He motioned for us to follow him without uttering a word. It was a replay of our departure from Tehran. Again I was shaking and pale with fear. In addition I was seriously ill. Our contact noticed my condition and firmly demanded that I exercise self-control. He shook hands with one of the customs officials and we passed through the gate without being stopped. He gave other guards the eye and we were whizzed through the other checkpoints. He gave us our boarding cards and told us not to move away from the final gate lest we miss the flight. The kind fellow told us that he had done all that he could for us and Javid shook his hand in thanks.

Within a few moments we were finding our seats on the plane in a state of both elation and fearful anticipation. I felt sad that my arms were empty of my little baby as I sat down in my assigned seat. Nonetheless, as I watched the luggage handlers load the plane a melody of joy rang in my heart as I thumbed through the pages of my memories of God's goodness. The seat belt sign illuminated and we all fastened our seat belts with thanksgiving in our souls. Our Lord had made a way through the high seas of Islamic bondage for us like Moses and the children of Israel when the Red Sea was parted for them. We were on our way to a better section of the wilderness on our long trek to our promised land.

Chapter 5

BLESSINGS IN MADRID

HELP FROM A FRIEND

Javid rang the call button for the flight attendant. She checked my temperature and expressed deep concern about its excessive level. She escorted us to the back of the plane and called over the public address system inquiring if there was a doctor aboard. A Swiss doctor responded and gave me as thorough an examination as the circumstances would allow. Fortunately, he had brought his medical bag on as carry-on luggage and was able to give me some medications to lower my fever and to reduce my dizziness. When he came to understand that we did not possess proper documents, he advised that we not mention my condition until after we had approached the passport zone after deplaning. He insisted that I seek immediate medical attention as soon as we were in Madrid. I awoke three hours later in time to be seated for our landing in Madrid's international airport.

In spite of the fact that I was ill, the group had no choice but to call upon me to converse with passport officials. Due to my private lessons, my English was better than theirs. The entrance official thought that I was kidding when I said that none of us had passports. He chuckled that no one approached his gate without passports in hand and again demanded to see ours. I again explained that we had none and that we were seeking political asylum in Spain. I then presented our Iranian birth certificates. The officer responded that no one sought asylum in

Spain and that, of all people, it was very unlikely that it would be granted to Iranians. He asked how long we planned to stay in Spain. Our nights without sleep prior to the flight began to take their toll. I was tired, sick and irritable, and with an intense tone in my voice, gave him our reasons for fleeing Iran by way of Turkey. All of us became upset when we learned that we had been sent to the wrong country for the purpose of asylum. The Turk who had arranged our flight was a conman. He simply got us the cheapest flight possible to the European continent so he could keep the balance for himself. He had absolutely no genuine concern for our welfare.

The official did not know what to do with us, so he sent us in to be interviewed by other officials. I had to rehearse our plight numerous times as we were passed from one office to the next. After three unbearable hours, Javid volunteered that I had experienced a miscarriage and was suffering from a severe abdominal infection. Then things began to move for us. They gave us permission to enter the country with the understanding that we must file our address so that they could contact us by mail. We were to receive a letter from the office of immigration that would notify us that we were to come in for an official interview. Meanwhile, Bita called an old friend who had immigrated to Madrid years before. Praise God that Bita had been inspired by the Holy Spirit to stay in contact with Shirin, her sister in the Lord. When we walked out into the airport's arrival hall, she was holding a sign with our names on it. After she repeatedly hugged Bita, the formal introductions were made and she got us a cab. Joyfully we drove to her apartment. As we drove along I was grateful to see that the streets of Madrid far surpassed those of Ankara in cleanliness. The people seemed to be happy as they conversed with one another at the sidewalk cafes. I thought to myself that free people even walk differently than those who live in oppression.

It was wonderful to enter a real home that was vermin free. The change in atmosphere was a godsend. Shortly after we arrived, Shirin's roommate walked in with a Farsi Bible in her hand. She introduced herself to us, and I told her that it was a marvel for us to see that someone could actually freely carry a Bible on the street. Then we all sat down and enjoyed the first substantial meal that we had eaten in months.

A REAL CHURCH

We had arrived on Saturday and Shirin took me to her Christian doctor that evening. He was not normally open at that late hour, but he made an exception for me. He gave me a thorough examination. He told me that he would have to prepare the proper medications for me at his home and would deliver them to me at the 2:00 p.m. Sunday service. He was sensitive to our circumstances and kindly did not charge me for the office visit and the prescriptions. I was to see him once a month until my condition improved. That night I slept in a wonderfully comfortable bed and was not awakened by any roaches crawling over me during the night. For me it was like a night in heaven.

On Sunday morning our hostesses prepared a marvelous breakfast for us, which they asked me to bless. I thanked the Lord for each stage of our deliverance and for giving us such faithful friends. While we ate the luscious meal, Shirin told us that we would need to be ready to depart for the church service in downtown Madrid at 1:00 p.m. Later on in the morning, Javid encouraged me to call my mother and give her Shirin's number in Madrid. He, along with I, believed that she would be relieved to learn that we were out of Turkey and that I was receiving proper medical attention. I was able to reach her and she sadly told me that no one was permitted to mention my name in the home of my youth. She promised to call when she had the opportunity to do so.

Our arrival was punctual at the ancient office building where the church services were held. It was our first experience of attending a public Christian meeting that did not have to be conducted in secret. There was actually a sign on the building signifying that it was the location of an Iranian church. The stairs that we climbed to get to the right floor did not seem to be completely reliable. Upon our entrance into the room, we saw around 40 fellow believers. Most were Iranians and the others were Afghanis and folks of European origins. They all had their heads bowed in prayer in preparation for the service. The tall, blond-haired, kind-featured pastor manned the organ, and he played beautifully.

The praise was exuberant as everyone clapped their hands and we enjoyed every moment of it. One of the songs that we sang from the hymnal was a favorite of mine titled, *Jesus Comes With All His Glory*. I was elated that I was no longer obligated to repeat the *salat* multiple times daily. The days of empty, dead, fear-filled religion were gone. I was now touching the heart of God as I worshipped Him in Spirit and in truth.

While I sang, the words of Pastor Soodmand appeared on the canvas of my heart: "When we sing it is actually a pure form of worship that is as valuable as hearing preaching in one's native tongue." Our group was pleasantly surprised when the non-Iranian pastor delivered his powerful sermon in flawless Farsi. The minister's trustable demeanor added to our being able to receive the full benefit of all that he said.

FORGIVENESS' RELEASE

His topic was forgiveness and his text was Luke 23:34. *Then Jesus said, "Father, forgive them, for they do not know what they do." And they divided His garments and cast lots.* I was deeply moved by the sermon and I really needed his admonishment that we all were to forgive, from the heart, those whom had hurt us. The floods of my heart broke forth and I arose from my seat and confessed that I wanted the ability to forgive and to be forgiven.

I prayed "I want to know Your peace and forgiveness, Lord. Jesus I need You, take my hand in Yours." The pastor laid his hand on my shoulder and led me in a prayer wherein I forgave all of those who had wronged me. Through that single act of forgiveness, the Holy Spirit performed a spiritual surgery within my soul. My bitterness toward the Islamic government of my nation for their hostile policy toward Christians was swept away. Though they had not made a formal apology for murdering Monir and forcing us into exile, my animosity for them vanished. My father had not called me to express his sorrow over saying that he rejected me. He had not phoned to encourage me by saying that I would always be his precious little girl regardless of my religion. Nonetheless, I was able to love him as though he had never disowned me and still experienced joy in hearing my voice. I requested baptism in water, as I had been unable to follow through with my planned baptism in Iran due to Monir's death. The pastor said that he would arrange it for a date in the near future. No one in the whole congregation had dry eyes as they rejoiced over what had taken place within me during that glorious service.

I cannot emphasize enough how important water baptism in the name of Jesus is for those from a background such as mine. It is not simply a ritual that permits one entrance into a particular denomination. It is a vital tool that makes the final separation from the bondages of one's old life. It gives one a sense of full identification with Jesus in His death, burial and resurrection. It also gives one the ability to truly walk as a new creation in Christ. When the devil comes knocking with old temptations and unforgiveness issues, he has no ground to play with. The person who had those issues is dead and buried in the name of the Father, the Son and the Holy Spirit. That is precisely what I anticipated would be my reward for obedience to the sacrament of baptism by immersion.

ANOTHER MARTYR

After the service we were invited to have tea at the home of an Iranian named Ahmed. While his wife prepared the refreshments, he showed us the photos of their family's water baptism there in Spain. I told him that I was blessed that he was living freely in Madrid and did not have to experience the injustices of Iran. He tearfully told us that his brother, who had led a

Tehran home group, had been executed the month before because he was a convert to Christianity.

My heart skipped beats as I asked his brother's name. None of us said a word when he arose and went to get pictures of his brother's family and their new baby girl. Inwardly, each of us prayed that it was not our Ali. He showed us the photos and we all gasped. Our Ali, the mighty soldier of the Cross, had been martyred like Monir. I felt that I might faint and slipped to a sitting position on the floor to avoid injuring myself if I fell. Ahmed told us that he had begged Ali to flee Iran on many occasions. It was sobering and humbling to know that he had valued his commitment to share his faith with us more that he had his own life. It was by God's grace that I had been filled with the Holy Spirit and had forgiven the Islamic officials the day that we heard about Ali's fate. If it were not for that, I would still be entrenched in a world of contemptuous distain for anyone connected with Iran's barbarous Islamic government.

TRIUMPH

We partially settled into life in Spain and it had significant contrasts with my life in Iran. At home I had never lacked anything. Our closets were full of expensive clothing. All we had in Spain was two sets of clothing each. We wore them on alternate days while the others were being washed. In Iran our home invariably had a fully stocked kitchen. In Madrid our cupboard was often bare. On numerous occasions our kind pastor delivered food to our door like manna in the wilderness. It was not unusual for us to drop in to visit Christian friends at mealtime simply because we had nothing to eat in our dwelling.

The Sunday of Javid's and my long-awaited water baptisms began with Satan's efforts to spoil the day. All we had to eat was two potatoes that I had opted to boil. While we were praying about the baptismal service, the pot boiled over and our lonely little potatoes were burnt to a crisp. The event did nothing to spoil our day. We were immersed along with 13 new converts. When we arose from our baptisms, all the bondages of Islam were floating dead and face down in the water. Ramadan, the Sharia, the call of muezzins from minarets, and the obligation to pray in Arabic while facing Mecca were washed away from the forefront of our memories. It would have been a disservice to our Lord to bring them back to mind. The Lord's presence became our constant companion. To this day our baptisms have remained one of the most treasured highlights of our Christian lives. We were inspired with fresh visions for our lives that have subsequently budded into fruition.

We experienced amazing spiritual growth under the tutelage of the pastor of Madrid's Iranian church. He was a father figure of wise council, as well as a spiritual leader, for all who came through the doors of his humble church. Our church was by no means a grand cathedral. It was in a dilapidated old building that had a leaky roof. It could never be said that the pastor was in it for the money. Most of the congregants were poor and the offering plate was often bare. Many hardly had enough money to take a bus to the services. Their financial statuses never hindered their spiritual enthusiasm for the things of God. It was a church filled with happy people who never failed to have lost souls on their hearts and praises on their lips.

RIVERS OF LIVING WATER

Prayer with fasting became an intermittent event in our lives. It was unlike the mandatory fast of Ramadan. We could choose to fast when the Spirit bade us to do so. Unlike some prideful Muslims, we did not fast as a performance before man like the Pharisees that Jesus mentioned in Matthew 6:16. – *"Moreover, when you fast, do not be like the hypocrites, with a sad countenance. For they disfigure their faces that they may appear to men to be fasting. Assuredly, I say to you, they have their reward."* The Muslim concept that God can be bought by missing 40 days of daytime meals and gorging at night was not within our thinking. We fasted to freshen our souls for the Lord's service and to receive new insights into His grace. I had come to Jesus begging for just one sip of joyous intimate fellowship with

God. He gave me a river of life that floods up from my soul (Jn. 4:14). It refreshes me and gives me the ability to give those that thirst for salvation a drink that turns into a perpetual river for them. It is wonderful not to have to teach people Islam's confession of faith when they are converted. Reciting, "I witness that there is no God but Allah and Muhammad is the messenger of Allah" brings spiritual death. The confession of Jesus as Lord brings the promise of answered prayers here on earth and eternity in heaven.

Christ gave me a new sense of self-esteem that was not rooted in the worldly pride that had influenced me when I was a Muslim girl from an affluent family. My pride did not stem from the fact that I had an influential father who was an expert in Islamic studies at one of the world's foremost Muslim universities. I no longer anticipated people noting me as the granddaughter of one of Iran's most renowned writers. I possessed a sense of divine destiny because my Heavenly Father is an expert in everything and is the author of the best-selling book of all time, and I will someday walk the streets of gold.

Javid and I were not rich in material things, but we praised God for the coming victories nonetheless. In the days when we had no money for heat and adequate nutrition, we learned that faith is the victory that overcomes the world. Christian victory demands the boldness to face life's adversities in faith. Victory is elusive for those who are timid and reserved about the things of God. It takes confidence in the reliability of God's unfailing Word to overcome what the devil throws at us in this life.

During one of the services at the Spanish church, I went forward when the pastor invited those who wanted special prayer to come to the altar. He asked what I wanted from God and I responded that I wanted to resume my studies so that I could serve God more effectively. I added that should I see my parents again I did not want to be shamed because I had not completed my education. Several days later he and his wife came to our dwelling with precious gifts in hand. They brought much needed foods for our pantry, but also something much more enduring. While we sipped our tea, they told us that God had whispered that they were to pay for our educations. Javid enrolled in Madrid's Bible University to get his theology degree and I enrolled in Madrid's English-speaking university. This was an absolute miracle that made us extremely happy.

A NESTING PLACE

There was a good Spanish-speaking evangelical church in Madrid that we occasionally attended. Its pastor owned a nice two-bedroom apartment, and he leased it to us for a very reasonable rent in comparison with the high prices of Madrid. We moved in with Reza and Bita and they both worked to help us all make ends meet. Four years after we arrived in Spain, they received papers to immigrate to Australia. They had tried to convince us to accompany them, but we did not sense that it was God's plan for our lives. Our parting was bittersweet. We were sad that our dear friends were departing from our daily times of fellowship, but we were glad that they were able to settle in a free western nation.

Before being taken to the airport by our pastor, Bita held my hand and reminded me of my promise to write her story someday. She had become like a sister to me, and it was heartrending when her hand slipped from mine for the final time. The apartment was lonely without their joyful presence. From time to time I would contact my mother or she would call me. That helped us keep some semblance of family while we were in our refugee status.

Our knowledge of the Lord and His Word grew by leaps and bounds when the pastor began a Bible study each Wednesday evening in our home. He took us through the entire Bible beginning with the book of Genesis. In the early years, the church had overflowed with people. Then more and more of the Iranians began to get work visas in other European nations. The practice was that the companies that were to employ them would pay their travel expenses. After they settled in their new residences they would pay their employers back through installment payments. It was a good thing for those immigrating, but it reduced our pastor's flock considerably. God's answer for this was to win more souls. That is where Javid and I played a pivotal role in the life of the fellowship.

While the Shah of Iran was in power, our government reluctantly allowed non-Islamic religions to function in Iran. During those years, our pastor had served there and developed a sincere love for Iranians. In addition, though he was British, he had learned to speak Farsi like a native, and his wife had learned to cook like an Iranian chef. On one of the many occasions that he and his wife prepared home-style dishes for us, he shared his vision for the church's future. The vision required our participation. He invited Javid to accompany him when he made house calls on prospective members and converts. We both began to go with him on evangelistic campaigns on the weekends. The Spaniards often remarked that we spoke Spanish like natives. Many came to the Lord and the church began to sparkle with the glory of enthusiastic new converts. It was a hands-on discipleship program that prepared us for the ministry to which the Lord had called us.

EXPULSION

We had been in Madrid for seven years, but we knew that it was not our permanent place. We prayed and asked the Lord for direction and we received a letter from the immigration office. The letter said that our visas would not be renewed and that we had to exit the country within ninety days. I read the letter and sat in shock on the staircase to our apartment. Where would we go and how would we get there? I phoned the pastor and told him about it and he came right over. He was visibly shaken and questioned how they could demand that we leave on such short notice after we had lived there for seven years. He shook his head in a mystified manner and said that we needed another letter to come in the mail saying, "Dear Mina, We cordially invite you to....Where?"

Javid became infuriated when I showed him the letter. We

had our studies, the church and our jobs. How could they expect us to just drop everything and leave because of some antiquated bureaucratic ruling? The pastor consulted a lawyer who told him that nothing could be done because Spain did not grant political asylum to anyone. This would be our third move and we had no idea where we would end up. For the next two months we increasingly felt pressure as the clock ticked toward the moment when we would either leave voluntarily or be forced out of the country.

During those hectic days, a Dutch missionary came to minister at our church. We invited him to our home for a luscious Iranian meal that he thoroughly enjoyed. As we fellowshipped after dinner he spontaneously asked the most unusual question: "Why don't you guys consider moving to the Netherlands?" We had never remotely thought about such a thing. The truth was we hardly knew anything about Holland except that it was famous for its tulips and was located somewhere in Northern Europe.

It was difficult for us to consider leaving Spain for numerous reasons. We played an important role in our church's evangelistic outreaches, we knew the language and our studies were progressing on schedule. And above all it was located close to Iran. In our hearts we were still hoping to go back there. If it were possible to return without risking our lives, we would run home at a moment's notice. However, regardless of our likes and dislikes, we had to take any option that opened before us. The whole church family agreed in prayer that God would guide us to make the right decision. The prospects of moving for a third time, learning a new language and living in a cold climate were not within our comfort zones. Naturally speaking, it was within our rights to desire to choose a country that was more familiar to us. But at the end of the day, God's will is always the best choice. His decision was that our next stop in our wilderness travels would be Holland.

The final week came and we had not yet made our travel arrangements. We were aware that procrastination could lead the immigration department to send the police to break into our apartment and to drag us to the airport. If that happened, we could find ourselves on a flight to anywhere, including Iran. We called the Dutch missionary who had invited us to his country, and he made the arrangements for our departure and arrival. We packed our clothes and books into two large suitcases and gave the rest of our belongings to the needy folks in our church. We were grateful that our move enabled them to have nice household furnishings. I called my mother to let her know about the upcoming change in our location. She questioned whether or not it was wise for us to leave Spain. I was able to convince her that it was a matter of necessity rather than a whim. She gave us her best wishes for a safe journey.

MORE GOODBYES

The ride to the airport was a little depressing for Javid and me. We were leaving all that we had called home and our spiritual family for the past seven years. It had been our assumption that the church in Madrid would be our home fellowship until the Lord allowed us to return to Tehran. With sad hearts we bade our dear pastor and his wife goodbye and boarded the plane. The most exhilarating thing about this departure was that we knew where we were going, that it was a Christianized nation and that loving people were excited about our coming. I looked out the plane's window and saw our beloved spiritual leader waving his hand at us as a final farewell gesture. We still glorify our King for every investment that the pastor contributed to our spiritual lives. He taught us the Word and how to fulfill our callings as evangelists to the Muslim global community. We had every intention of holding him to his promise to visit us in the cold weather of Holland. Javid and I looked at one another as the plane ascended and knew that we had the same question in our hearts. Why did the Lord want us in the Netherlands?

Chapter 6

KIDNAPPED

NETWORK OF GLORY

Our plane made a smooth landing in Amsterdam, Holland, and we deplaned following the other passengers to the passport desk. Unlike the others, we did not know what would befall us. The first thing that we noted about the people in the airport was that they were all bundled in warm clothing. We deduced that we were about to experience our first taste of Northern Europe's cold climate. I could never fathom that I was about to meet a person who had anonymously blessed me in the past and was about to bless me again.

The officer at the passport control station addressed us in Dutch. We did not understand a word that he said, so I switched into the international language, English. Speaking very softly, I explained that we were seeking political asylum from Iran. He jerked his head up and loudly said, "Oh, asylum. You will have to go to the immigration department and give them your reasons for seeking asylum." It was a little embarrassing to have the other passengers stare at us as though they had never previously seen refugees. We were ushered into the correct office and held there for 10 hours.

They brought in a friendly Iranian lady to serve as our interpreter while they questioned us. She stared at me all during the interview and I returned her stare thinking that she looked vaguely familiar. She seemed to light up when I gave our testimonies as the reason for our needing residence in Holland. She inquired, "Haven't I seen you somewhere before?"

My response was, "I was thinking the same thing about you. I know that I have seen you previously, but I cannot imagine where it was." Then I continued on with the account of my conversion.

I came to the part of my testimony about how I found the Farsi Bible in the university library and tears began to stream down her face. She rose to her feet and spoke to me in Farsi while holding her face with her hands with an expression of amazement.

"I am the person who placed that Bible beneath the desk and I was the librarian who insisted that you take it home and read it." She hugged me and spoke in Dutch to the officer explaining that which she had just told me. I marveled at the manner in which the Holy Spirit had kept us in a network of interrelated people all through our Christian adventures. I found a Bible and Monir passed out Bibles. Pastor Soodmand who led me to Christ had also led Monir and my husband to the Lord. Javid and I both attended prayer meetings in Ali's home, but on different nights. The day that we met Ahmad in Spain we discovered that he was the brother of Ali who had been executed. Now I was in the embrace of a woman in Amsterdam who was the very person who had placed the Bible in the library in Tehran. The Holy Spirit is the Wonder of all wonders! Best of all, the officer was very impressed and commented that its a small world as he stamped our papers permitting us entrance into Holland.

We waited on the missionary who had invited us to Holland, but he never showed up. The woman who had been interpreting for us spotted us waiting for him in the arrival hall. She again blessed us by inviting us to stay with her family until we could get settled. That night we blessed the Lord for preparing the way for us. We were exhausted from the excitement of all that had transpired, and it was wonderful to rest comfortably in a warm and friendly home.

TAKE HIM TO THE STREETS

We eventually got our own place and Javid resumed his theological studies at Amsterdam's university. We both became very burdened for the salvation of the many Muslims that wandered the streets of the city. They had come from all over the Middle East to seek economic opportunities that were nonexistent in their homelands. These refugees were so vast in number that the Dutch government had to establish camps to house them at various sites throughout the nation. We prayed and fasted for forty days and the Lord revealed to us that the Muslims of the Netherlands were our mission field and that it was ripe for harvest.

It soon became clear that God had uniquely guided our lives in a manner that gave us full qualifications to minister to the Muslim community. Through first-hand experience we knew the dark regulations of their fanatical religion. We spoke multiple languages: Farsi, Arabic, English and Spanish and were quickly picking up Dutch. Most importantly, we had the answer for the ultimate need of their lives: Jesus. The Holy Spirit led many wonderful people to assist us in evangelistic campaigns that we held in the refugee camps. In 1990 we launched into full-time ministry under the name, *Touch of Christ Ministries*.

Most of our evangelistic efforts, and the weekly Bible studies that we established, were concentrated among the Muslims who spoke one of three languages: Arabic, Farsi and Urdu. At times it took four to five hours to reach the camps, but our efforts were well rewarded. Our backgrounds as former Muslims caused them to trustingly welcome us into their makeshift homes to hear what we had to say. Numerous detainees had become addicted to drugs, and the Lord gifted us with the power to liberate them from their bondages.

One such fellow was an Iranian named Hataf whom we had invited to our home for a meal. It turned out that he had turned to the Lord two weeks after fleeing Iran. As we conversed with him after dinner, his heroin addiction compelled him to begin to act erratically and to shake convulsively. We offered to take him to the detoxification unit of the hospital, but he refused. He just wanted to leave so he could get the fix that he was craving.

He angrily lashed out at us, "I don't want your friendship. Just leave me alone and let me out of here." The Lord led us to ignore his demands and to lay hands on him and pray that his pains and shaking would subside. Our prayers filled the room with the name of Jesus and intensified his anger. All he could do was to cry like a wounded child complaining that the pain was killing him. Though he had been a believer for about a month, he had no idea that God had the power to nullify drug addiction. He told us that he loved Jesus, but he wanted us to stop praying so that he could leave.

Suddenly, he pointed his shaking hand heavenward, "Javid, I see a huge hand coming toward me and now I can feel it touching me. It's the hand of Jesus. Hallelujah! Hallelujah! Jesus, heal me now. All the pain and shaking is gone, I can't believe that this is my body. Javid hit me hard on the leg. I want to see if it is actually my leg that has stopped shaking." His body relaxed and he bowed his head to the floor sobbing in gratitude to the Lord for his deliverance. We knew that it was best that he be isolated from his old companions in the drug scene. Hataf stayed with us four months and became a very strong believer.

ASSASSINATION THWARTED

Farhad was not as addicted to drugs. He was addicted to thoughts of murderous hatred. His mission in Holland was not the pursuit of economic security. He had come all the way from an Iranian Kurdish village to avenge the rape of his sister. He had vowed that he would kill the man who had shamed his family and then leave the country. He heard us proclaiming the love of Christ and rushed out of the camp's evangelistic center sobbing under the conviction of the Holy Spirit. We followed him out and he told us his story. He also showed us the knife that he planned to shove into the body of the man who was guilty of the rape. We brought him back into the center and he knelt in front of the wooden cross that we had placed on the altar.

"Jesus, I beg You to clean this bitterness from my heart. I know that my family will criticize me for not fulfilling my murderous mission, but I just can't do it. Javid, take this knife from me and throw it away. It will not be a bloodstained dagger that I take back to my village to brandish before my relatives. I will show them this Bible that you have given to me. It is my plan to take the message of the love of Jesus to the poor captives of Islam in my hometown." With that, he fell into Javid's prayerful embrace. The next day he phoned to tell us that he was on the way back to his village with Jesus in his heart and the Good News of God's forgiveness on his lips.

Full-time ministry among the Muslims was a difficult task that took nearly 24 hours per day, seven days each week. Nonetheless, we were invigorated by the results that God was granting us. It was exhilarating to see pride-filled Muslim men humbled by the impartation of the love of Jesus. It was wonderful to know that they would no longer obey Muhammad's instructions to beat their wives for the slightest offense (Koran 4:34). The liberty of the Lord elevates ex-Muslim daughters and wives to honored positions that they could never experience under Islam.

Another of the many examples that signaled that Javid and I were on the right track was the conversion of a fourteen-year-old Kurdish boy, named Ahwad, in one of the camps. He bravely raised his hand in response to Javid's invitation for those who wanted to accept Christ. The other Muslims later criticized his decision and tried to convince him that he was only a child and far too young to make such a decision. He forcefully challenged the accuracy of their assessment.

"How can you dare call me a child? I never knew a real childhood. My mother cut my umbilical cord with a dirty knife when I was born and my only toys were guns. I was raised among the rough youths of the mountains who never owned any of the harmless toys that most children play with. We carried guns and fought alongside the older Kurds. I don't qualify as a child by anyone's standards."

WRITING BEGINS AND A CHURCH IS BORN

During our time in Amsterdam there were two contacts that we maintained in Iran, my mother and Pastor Soodmand. I intermittently called my mother just to hear her voice and to assure her that we were doing well and had not forgotten her. We called our beloved pastor to report our progress and to receive his encouragement. He occasionally reminded Javid that his prophetic word about him was in the process of being fulfilled.

"The first time that I laid eyes on you in that Meshhad farm house, didn't I tell you that you would someday be a mighty soldier in the Lord's army?" he asked.

We both grieved deeply when, shortly after our arrival in December of 1990, we heard that he had been mercilessly executed by the Ayatollah's regime. We got the long-distance call from Mahtab in Iran while we were conducting a meeting. Upon hearing of his death, I fell to the floor weeping with the phone still in my hand. I momentarily regretted that I no longer had the option of hating his Islamic executioners. I had no choice but to forgive them as Christ had forgiven me. We did not have the emotional resources to continue the meeting that night. We dismissed the people after telling them that it had been an honor to come to the Lord through such a humble servant of the Cross. Everyone praised God for his years of sacrifices for those imprisoned by Islam.

I tearfully moped around our apartment for days, until the Lord spoke to me one night: "Why are you crying? Don't use your energy spilling tears over someone who is with Me. Use your energies to write about all that I have done for your lives. Instead of all your tears, write what I have done for you!"

My obedience to His voice cured my grief and resulted in the writing of *Don't Keep Me Silent*. I titled it that because I could not be silent about the 70 million Muslims who were perishing without Christ in Iran, and the 1 billion-plus who are living else-where. I was compelled to offer them the only solution, Jesus, for the battles against human dignity that raged against all who put their trust in Muhammad's Allah. It was published in Dutch and proved to be a blessing for thousands. The publishers asked for permission to publish it in a total of six languages. We used the profits to print children's Bibles in Kurdish to distribute among kids who had never even held a Bible.

In 1993 we planted Amsterdam's first Farsi-speaking church in the heart of the city. Hundreds of Iranian and Afghani refugees were brought to the throne of grace in our small church. Those were busy and productive days. Javid pastored the fellowship and we both participated in our weekly Bible studies at the camps. We also evangelized on Amsterdam's street corners through the use of a megaphone. Few natives of the city exhibited any interests in spiritual matters. It was gratifying when Dutch folks, as well as Muslims, stopped to hear our street-corner worship and messages about the Lord. Dutch churches began to invite us to share our testimonies. We never failed to accept the invitations. We wanted to challenge people with the plight of Muslims who were living under miserable restrictions in their efforts to please Allah.

It was not unusual for Muslim extremists to enter these services and attempt to disrupt what we were saying. On one occasion we were speaking to a congregation of two thousand and two radical Muslims accosted us. One of them grabbed the book from my hand and screamed at me as he tore it to shreds, "Why are you blaspheming, you infidel?" The ushers escorted them both from the service. When Javid and I exited after the service, they were waiting for us and made threats on our lives. Our response was sorrow for their blindness, and we prayed for them. We understood that if it were not for the mercy of God, we could have been fanatics who disrupted services. We were not deterred one iota by their threats.

Incidents like this, and the success of *Don't Keep Me Silent*, inspired me to write a paper titled *A Journey Through The Koran*.

It exposed the errors of the Koran. I knew that a portion of my mission from the Lord was to nullify the misconceptions that the Koran fostered in the hearts and minds of Muslims. I didn't complete the project until 1997. Our funds had been exhausted by the Kurdish Bible project and we could not publish the paper in booklet form. We ran off 10,000 copies on a copier and distributed them to hungry souls. This project was completed shortly after I experienced a harrowing encounter with kidnappers.

Threatening phone calls had begun to come into our home. We changed our phone number numerous times and the calls continued. This confirmed our worst fears: Muhammad's zealots were relentlessly successful at tracking us down. Three nights after one of these calls, a drunken man came to our door at 11:00 p.m. and incessantly banged on it to gain entrance. He cursed Christians and the Bible for 30 minutes in flawless Farsi. I was not about to let him in without Javid's presence in our home. He was visiting a parishioner's home that evening. I thought that the violator could have been feigning drunkenness and might have actually been an Iranian secret agent. I phoned the police and they were not impressed by my pleas. He eventually left on his own accord shortly before Javid returned home. That event put us on our guard. We became apprehensively aware that no matter how effective we were for the Lord, we were not safe in Holland.

THE ABDUCTION

Two nights later I was making the ten-minute walk down the dark street from the metro station to our apartment. It was 9:30 p.m. and I sensed that I was being followed. I was in the process of passing a mysterious car that had pulled alongside of me and then parked at the curb. The doors swung open and two men jumped out and violently shoved me into its backseat. My Bible and research papers fell onto the street and one of them picked them up before we sped away. I quickly saw that there were four of them, two younger men, an older driver and a woman.

Years of familiarity with Islamic teachings led me to understand that there are abundant Koranic texts that sanctioned torture and death for those, such as me, who are regarded as apostates. One of the young men attempted to subdue my screams by slapping me with full force in the face. The woman disdainfully, repeatedly called me a dirty *kafar* infidel as she taped my mouth shut. One of the front-seat passengers uttered words that chilled my bones and almost caused me to slip into a faint: "You must die."

My mind swirled with the irony of it all. I had eluded Iran's Muslim thugs only to die in a free society by the hands of its Muslim thugs. It would have been far more preferable to die for Christ in my homeland. Why did I have to come all the way to Europe to be assassinated? As we drove though the darkness, the woman kept jerking me by the hair and yelling for me to repent of my apostasy. I could not scream because of the tape over my mouth. When she did not see me nodding my head in compliance she became even more infuriated.

After a lengthy drive the car pulled up in front of a dilapidated old house. They hastily dragged me from the car and we entered the filthy house that had boxes scattered throughout it. Two of the men remained upstairs. The other guy and the woman shoved me into the basement. They took turns battering me. She pulled my hair and slapped me. He threw me from one wall to the other. All the while they were demanding my repentance. Even if I had tried to answer, the sound would have not gotten past the tape over my mouth. They assured me that I was going to die one way or the other, but they wanted to give me as much pain as possible before my death.

The ruffian poked his finger under my nose saying, "When are you going to renounce Christianity? Will it be now or later? You dirty animal, tomorrow you will be joining your Christian friends who have died and gone to hell." He gave me another stunning blow to the face, then he closed the door and they went upstairs.

The voice of one of them who was conversing with a superior by phone drifted down within my hearing. "*Hajji* (holy man) it is done. We will finish the job tomorrow." I heard their steps exiting the house and the door being closed. My prison was silent except for the sound of my muffled sobs. I was devastated by the whole matter and prayed that God would just let me die alone before they came back to torture me to death. I had never felt so helpless and could gather no confidence that I would be rescued. All through the night my head would jerk as I awoke only to find that I was still on the floor of that terribly cold and damp basement. The next morning I heard them reenter the house and also heard voices that were unfamiliar to me. They made and received numerous phone calls. Every hour one of them would come down and taunt me about my impending doom. They would tear pages from my Bible and throw them at my head. They wanted to brainwash every ounce of faith in Christ from my being. I expected a knife to slash my throat or a gunshot to pierce my heart at any moment. I cannot deny that I was fearful of the manner in which they would execute me. In desperation, I began to call upon the name of Jesus afresh for my deliverance. I vowed to serve Him faithfully if I was liberated from that awful predicament.

HOPE AGAINST HOPE

The third night the old driver appeared, un-taped my mouth and gave me a glass of water. I thought that the water was likely poisoned, but went ahead and drank it. Death by poison would be quicker than through torture.

While he re-taped my mouth he instructed me to run away as fast as I could after I heard everyone leave the house: "I cannot do anything further for you except to leave the door unlocked for your escape." I thought that it might be another mind game, but decided to risk running upstairs and out the door anyway. I hovered in the dark until it was safe to make my run. Surely an angel helped me get up the stairs and out the door. The speed of my running would have shamed the fastest running champion on earth. The cold snow crunched under my bare-feet and the pain was so intense that it was barely tolerable to continue running. The cold, blowing wind nearly took my breath away. I flagged down a car and it stopped. The Dutchman opened the door for me with a hesitant hint of fright in his voice. He kindly drove me to the nearest police station. Javid and some of the other believers rushed there to assist me home. The entire congregation had been frantically looking for me for two days.

We filed a complaint with the police, but they warned that they were powerless to stop religiously incited attacks on refugees. I leaned against Javid and shook with fright. The police suggested that our only permanent solution was to flee to another country. The thought of leaving the fruitful ministry that the Lord had given us was heartbreaking. How could we abandon the souls who looked to us for leadership? While pondering our decision we hid in the home of another Christian for several days. It was as though some sort of sign was tattooed upon our foreheads that made us targets for persecution. We both knew that our only option was to flee. Inwardly I knew that though we could flee to another country, it was impossible to outdistance the death threats of militant Muslims.

Javid and I fasted and prayed for 72 hours about where we should go. During that time the Lord spoke the name of a city to Javid: Washington, D.C. Unlike most people from the Middle East, we had never had a desire to come to America. We wanted to stay in a close geographical proximity to Iran in case the doors swung open there. We did not suspect that the God of our salvation had plans for us in the United States. Miraculously, within 10 days of the moment that Javid got the name of America's capitol, we were on a flight to New York. The immigration authorities of America understood religious persecution, and graciously granted us the asylum that we had sought for years. God had opened another pass for us through the wilderness. We sensed that we were embarking on our final trek to our promised land.

Chapter 7

SIGNS & WONDERS

REMINISCING

It was 4:30 p.m. on a day in March of 1998, and Javid and I were on our flight from Amsterdam to New York. I could not help feeling like a fish out of water as the plane was filled with mostly Americans and Europeans and only a few people from the Middle East. I had accepted the Savior that many in the West claim, but I had never become comfortable with their Western lifestyles. I had not traveled to the U.S. and it would have been my preference to remain in Europe. The rumors that I had heard about Americans' lifestyles were not particularly appealing to me. Of course, my primary dream was ever in my thoughts: to return to Iran.

In the quiet seclusion of my seat, memories flooded into my mind of all that I had missed since my conversion. I longed to gaze upon my mother's lovely face and to sit at her sumptuous table with my entire family. I would have given anything to see my father's wrinkled hands holding one of his study books. Above all, I prayed that somehow the Spirit of God would permeate the evil cloud of Islam that surrounded them and that they would confess Jesus as Lord. It was also my prayer that God would decrease the time that was allotted for us to remain in exile.

The Islamic government had deeply wounded me, but the hope of eventually preaching to Muslims in my homeland was foremost in my heart. At times I asked the Lord to either let me return to Iran or to release me from my burden for the salvation of her people. In those moments I felt that the best years of my life had been spent in separation from those who I valued so highly. Birthdays, anniversaries and holiday's were particularly difficult for Javid and me to spend alone. The Lord had blessed us with a spiritual family filled with loving Christians. They were wonderful, but they did not fulfill our needs to be around our earthly families. It seemed that our whole lives were busied with either running to or from somewhere or something. I snapped out of my daydreams. I came back to the reality that we were moving to our fourth nation and again with nothing but a single suitcase each.

It was unsettling to leave all that we had built behind us. Satan had robbed us of the opportunity to fully enjoy the fruit of our labors among those who had formerly been his captives. That thief had stolen portions of the peace and joy we had garnered over the eight years that we lived in Amsterdam. The Bible says that a thief has to restore that which he has stolen sevenfold. Perhaps the Lord had something in store for us in the U.S. that would fulfill that promise. Knowing God, it had to be something marvelous.

VISIONS FROM THE THRONE

I noticed that Javid was highlighting passages in his Bible as he sat beside me. "Are you getting any revelations about where we will end up after this plane lands?" I asked him.

He looked at me with heaven-born confidence. "I don't know all of the details about how or where it will happen, but I do know that God will take care of us." We both took confidence in the fact that our next stop was the freest nation on earth. It would be a joy to work for our King in an environment that was not clouded by religious persecution.

I was deep in contemplation about where we would spend our first night in America when Javid interrupted me, "Mina, listen to this passage. There is something in it that pertains to our first days in America." Acts 12:7-10 - *Now behold, an angel*

136

of the Lord stood by him, and a light shone in the prison; and he struck Peter on the side and raised him up, saying, "Arise quickly!" And his chains fell off his hands. [8] Then the angel said to him, "Gird yourself and tie on your sandals"; and so he did. And he said to him, "Put on your garment and follow me." [9] So he went out and followed him, and did not know that what was done by the angel was real, but thought he was seeing a vision. [10] When they were past the first and the second guard posts, they came to the iron gate that leads to the city, which opened to them of its own accord; and they went out and went down one street, and immediately the angel departed from him.

Javid excitedly told me that the Holy Spirit had given him a vision of something that we would see after we had deplaned in New York. The vision and the verses that accompanied it would be fulfilled on the streets of the city. The glory of God gleamed from his face and I knew that he was having a divine encounter. Four hours remained in the flight and I decided to also turn to my Bible. It was the best prescription that I could apply to my heart whenever I felt down or lonely for my family.

My Bible was opened on my lap, but I was not really concentrating on that which I read. I thought a little coffee would perk me up so I rang the attendant and asked her to bring me a cup. The American lady who was sitting in our row passed the coffee to me and started conversing with me. Javid joined in the conversation and we told her about the love of Christ. I told her that she had more opportunities to learn about Jesus than most anyone, because she resided in a Christianized nation that had thousands of churches.

Soon the plane was landing. She asked us where we planned to stay after our arrival in New York. She thought we were kidding when we said that we had no idea where we would be staying.

She cautioned us that it usually took quite a while for immigrants to pass the immigration area. She kindly gave us her address and phone number along with two bottles of spring water. She was the first American for whom we had the opportunity to pray. We had learned on the plane that she had a thirty-year-old daughter who suffered with bouts of depression. Right there in the airport terminal we joined hands with her and agreed in prayer that her daughter would be emotionally restored. She thanked us for the kind gesture and bade us farewell.

GATES OPEN

After two hours in the line we finally came face to face with an immigration officer who was checking the passports. He looked us over and asked how long we were planning to stay in America. I said, "Until the day there is freedom in our land!" He smiled and examined our documents. "Your papers are actually incomplete for legal entrance into America. But, you are welcomed to the U.S.A. anyway."

As we passed through the gate, Javid reminded me of the word that he had received on the plane from the book of Acts. It had inferred that we would be supernaturally guided around governmental complications. He also let me know that he had received a word of knowledge about a man that we would be meeting on the streets of New York. In a vision he had seen several men selling fruits from a cart. The Lord spoke to him that he was to give the one named George the message of salvation through Christ.

We passed through the final large, metal door of the busiest airport in the world and were standing on American soil. We were exhausted from travel, but it had been a cakewalk in comparison to our donkey rides over the cold mountains of Iran's Kurdish area on the way to Turkey. The other passengers from our flight passed us on their way to their homes and families. We just stood outside the terminal with our suitcases in our hands wondering what we were to do next. I took out my phone diary and found the number of a wonderful retired minister who had been recommended to us by a trusted friend. It was 2:00 in the morning and I was a little hesitant to call someone that I did not know. However, the circumstances demanded that I overcome my timidity and make the call. We found a phone booth and needed change to make the call. All we had was $300 in cash and all of the concessions were closed for the night. A man passed by and asked if we needed a quarter for the phone. He kindly gave us the coin and I made my call. Unfortunately there was no answer and the machine kept the quarter. I became agitated that simple things could become so complicated. We did not welcome the prospects of sleeping in the airport that night. Javid scurried off to find another coin. He returned victorious and I dropped the coin into the slot. The old minister answered the phone and I introduced myself. He had a weak voice, was hard of hearing and did not have a clue about who we were. He said that we must have the wrong number and started to hang up. I begged him not to and explained that we were ex-Muslim Christian ministers who had flown in from Holland. When he heard that we had no place to stay he invited us to take a cab to his home. We blessed the Lord for giving us a place to stay that first night in the States.

His apartment was in the heart of the city. Javid gave the cab driver the piece of paper that had our destination on it. Javid whispered to me that our beginnings in America might be trying, "In the Lord, trials often pave the way for great blessings. Just you wait and see, God has terrific plans for us."

The driver studied us through his rearview mirror and inquired, "Are you tourist or do you live here?" Without waiting for an answer he spouted, "Life here in America can be very difficult."

Throughout the ride I was astonished to see that New York was a city that never slept. At 3:00 a.m. the streets were bustling with activity. We arrived at the apartment building and rode the elevator to the 22nd floor. The minister met us halfway down the hall and kissed us as though he had treasured us for years. He welcomed us into his one bedroom flat that had a magnificent view of Manhattan. He was kindly caring, but I was too shy to let him know that I was famished from hunger.

VISION FULFILLED

Right after our arrival, Javid went out to get a phone card so we could let our friends in Europe know that we had arrived safely. The minister pointed out the highlights of the city for me that could be seen from his window. Javid returned with a wonderful praise report. He had met the George whom he had seen in his vision. He and another fellow were attending a fruit-wagon concession stand. The man had been shocked that Javid knew his name and was therefore very open to the Gospel message that Javid gave him. George told Javid that he had lived beside a church for 10 years, but had never set foot in it. He was so touched by the presence of the Lord that beamed through Javid's demeanor that he accepted Christ right there in the street. We had been in America less than 24 hours and the Lord had already begun to give us the first fruits of our ministry. Subsequently, we kept in contact with George, and after two years of agreeing in prayer, his gang-member son came to the Lord. He and his father are now active members in the church next to their home that they once ignored.

The minister's rollaway bed was not particularly comfortable. Nonetheless we slept as though we were in the arms of angels. The next morning we were awakened by the sounds of beeping horns from the streets below. During breakfast, Javid told the old fellow that we needed to get to Washington, D.C. as soon as possible. He looked at us and asked why it had to be as soon as possible. "I thought you said that you did not know anyone in America!" he said. He was deeply touched when Javid gave him the account of how he had received the name of the city that we were to settle in during our three-day fast in Holland. He encouraged us to settle in New York, but we gently insisted that our place was Washington. When he understood that we had to go there to remain in God's plan, he gave us the name of someone who could meet us at the train station. According to Iranian customs he graciously paid our cab fare, kissed us goodbye and sent us on our way to the train depot.

ANGELIC ASSISTANCE

We were waiting in the line to purchase our tickets. A tall, white-haired fellow, who was elegantly dressed in white from head-to-foot, cut in line ahead of the others. Curiously, no one objected. I could not take my eyes off of him. The next thing I knew, he was smiling down at us with two tickets in his hand, "I have paid for your tickets and please accept them as my gift." Javid and I looked at him in amazement. We were accustomed to the miracles of God, but this event was highly unusual. He smiled and handed Javid the tickets and walked away. Javid and I were dumbfounded. Who was he? Was he an angel from God? Javid ran in the direction that he had taken, assuming that he could easily be spotted again due to his height and his regal white attire. He had vanished. It was obvious to us that he was the angel of the Lord who was watching over us. This was another confirmation that we were progressing in the path of God.

We boarded the train to Washington and Javid immediately got his Bible out and began to pray. The train was almost empty of passengers and I passed the time enjoying the scenery from the window. We didn't converse with one another, as we were both still astonished by what had occurred during our first hours in the States. A fulfilled vision and an angelic visitation would give anyone something to think about. I sent praises up to my Lord by softly singing Monir's favorite song, *He is Lord*. In spite of all the difficulties that we had experienced, we were proud that we were the children of God and beneficiaries of His unmerited favor. Javid broke the silence, "Didn't I tell you that God would take care of us?"

GOD LOVES MUSLIMS

During our first 18 months in Washington we held two weekly Bible studies in the homes of the participants. On Wednesdays we ministered to those who spoke Arabic and on Thursdays to those who spoke Farsi. Before long, vibrant new converts from Islam filled the homes to overflow capacity. This led us to open Virginia's first Farsi-speaking church in September of 1999. We also maintained our ministry of evangelizing Muslims through the *Touch of Christ Ministries* that we had founded in Holland in 1990. Through it we brought many Arabic-speaking Muslims to the Lord and our church was mightily used to bring Iranians out of Islam's wilderness. We rejoiced in the fact that Satan's kingdom was being shattered by the number of people who were being delivered from Islam's talons.

Javid never failed to seek opportunities to evangelize. One day we were on our way to a prayer session with an Afghani family and we had to stop for a red traffic light. He noticed that the people in the car in the lane next to us were Arabs, as the woman was wearing a veil. He leaped from the car, introduced himself and attempted to give them an Arabic Bible. The man was a radical Saudi who led the prayers at his mosque, and he refused the Bible. Horns were blasting away at us because the light had turned green. To get Javid off of his back he reluctantly took the Bible and our phone number. One week later we found that he had left a message for us on our answering machine to give him a call. He sounded rather depressed so Javid responded quickly. With his voice choking with sobs he introduced himself as Ahmad, the man who had taken the Bible at the red light. He explained that his wife, Fatima, was dying of catastrophic lung cancer and had asked him to call us. The cancer was spreading through her entire body and he urged us to come to his home.

GOD HEALS MUSLIMS

The moment we entered their house we sensed the malignant presence of the spirit of death. Fatima began to weep and told us that she was very worried about who would care for her youngsters if she died. She explained that Ahmad's family had treated her badly and that she would not entrust her children to them. Javid sweetly told her of Jesus' compassionate love for her and her children. He read Mark 1:40-42 to her and told her that the

Lord was willing to heal her just as he had the leper. All she need do was to ask Him to do so as the leper had. - *Now a leper came to Him, imploring Him, kneeling down to Him and saying to Him, "If You are willing, You can make me clean." [41] Then Jesus, moved with compassion, stretched out His hand and touched him, and said to him, "I am willing; be cleansed." [42] As soon as He had spoken, immediately the leprosy left him, and he was cleansed.*

Fatima immediately responded, "I am like that leper. I want Jesus to cleanse me from cancer." Javid asked for permission to pray for her and she said that she was dying and that asking permission was unnecessary. We anointed her with oil and began to pray for her with heartfelt faith.

She cried out repeatedly, "Oh, God help me, heal me." The manifest presence of the Holy Spirit could be sensed in that room, and the spirit of death vanished. That encouraged us to pray with even more zeal. The following day she was scheduled for major surgery. They doubted that the operation would yield positive results. We promised to keep praying for her and walked out the door leaving her looking pale. We were only a few steps away when we head her shouting. "God, oh God, I'm healed. You are in this house and I don't even deserve healing. Thank you, thank you God."

We rushed back in to see what had happened. The entire home and Fatima's face glistened with the radiance of Christ. Ahmad was ecstatic as he told us that something wonderful entered the house when we walked out the door. A divine personage had walked into the room carrying candelabras in each hand. He spoke directly to Fatima telling her that they were for the celebration of her healing. He lit one of them and the room was illuminated with a blinding glory.

"Fatima, do you know Me? I am the one who heals and you are healed." Then she heard what seemed to be thousands of voices shouting hallelujah. Javid asked if she wanted to give her heart to Jesus, her Healer. She said yes without looking at her husband. Muslim women who give their hearts to Christ can suffer severe spousal abuse.

"I saw Him with my own eyes," she said. "Earlier when you were speaking about Him I was inwardly praying. I told Jesus that I wanted to give my heart to Him and belong to Him. I didn't say anything about it for fear of how Ahmad might react."

We joined hands with her and led her in the sinners' prayer. She gave her life to the Lord while her husband gave thanks to Allah. That night we prayed all night thanking God for her healing and her surgery that was scheduled for the next day. We kept our word and met them at Inova Hospital in Fairfax, Virginia, the following morning at 7:00. Javid told them that we believed she was healed regardless of what the physicians might say. He confidently promised her that she was healed. It was the beginning of a challenging day for everyone.

They arrived with Ahmad's sister accompanying them. Both she and Fatima were veiled and Fatima did not want to acknowledge our presence in front of her. The nurses had her fill out the release forms and took her in for the pre-operation tests. The doctor came in and she asked him about the results of the tests. He said that there had been no changes. She looked at us with her eyes saying, "I know I was healed."

Javid whispered, "Fatima, trust Jesus. Believe that He has healed you."

Ahmad's sister had surmised that we were Christians and stared at us contemptuously. She ordered us out of the room. She could not tolerate any mention of the name of Jesus. We started out of the room and Fatima asked us to stay and to pray for her healing before the surgery. Her sister-in-law tried again to dismiss us from the room. Fatima mustered her strength and firmly told her that she wanted us to pray for her one last time. With that, her sister-in-law left the room in a huff.

As we laid our hands on her, she asked, "What happened to my healing that came during the visitation from Jesus Christ? I'm sure that He told me that I was healed. How could I now be minutes away from surgery?"

Javid looked at her tenderly and said, "Fatima, have faith."

The physicians came into the room as Fatima was praising the Lord for her healing while we prayed for her. One of them commented that prayer was needed because the cancer was rapidly spreading. They wheeled her into the surgical unit and we stayed with Ahmad while he wept in the waiting room.

He confided in us that he believed that the hurts that his family had caused Fatima could be the reason for her cancer. It is a customary thing for Arabs who dislike someone to put curses upon them. He then began to question us about her healing. "Do you think she is really healed?"

Javid said, "With all of my faith in Christ I can say yes, she is healed."

"Then why is she now in surgery?"

"Ahmad, the Lord is teaching both of you a lesson about faith that you might not learn unless she entered that operating room."

As they spoke, the doctor rushed out of the unit. Ahmad asked him what was happening.

He answered, "Please wait, we are not sure about just what is happening."

Javid and I followed on his heels and he turned and firmly told us that we would have to wait for him to check some things.

Ahmad's sister saw all the commotion and announced, "Fatima is dead!"

Javid looked her square in the eyes. "No, she is not. Fatima is alive and healed."

She angrily spat, "Can't you stop talking about this Jesus? It is you who has brought all of these problems on my poor brother."

Ahmad told her to stop talking, but she raved on, "If you stay in contact with these Christians, I will renounce you as being my brother." While she hissed like a cobra the doctor entered the waiting room with a smile on his face.

He spoke with excited shortness of breath. "Your prayers have been answered. We ran some final tests in the operating room and our scalpels were poised to open her up. The tests all came back negative. We found absolutely no malignancy anywhere in her body. This is indeed a miracle. Before she went into the surgical unit her tests today indicated that she was full of cancer. Less than an hour later, in the operating room, the same tests showed that she has no cancer. The only explanation is that God healed her before we could insert our scalpels into her body."

Ahmad's sister looked at the doctor like he was an enemy. Ahmad asked, "Are you sure that she has no cancer?"

He answered, "A few hours ago she did, now three highly technical tests that are known for their accuracy indicate that she is completely cancer free."

I lifted up my hands in praise and Javid fell to his knees and thanked the Lord for His wonder-working power.

The physician volunteered, "I have worked in this hospital for 37 years and have never seen anyone kneel down on the floor and praise God." The sister-in-law was not pleased. It is possible that she would rather have seen Fatima go through surgery than to see Jesus get the glory for her healing. She did not want her brother to become interested in becoming a despicable Christian.

They transferred Fatima to another room and we rushed to be there when she awoke from the anesthesia. We had to apologize for pushing our way onto the elevator. The three physicians came into her room and confirmed that all of their tests revealed that she was a miracle woman. They expressed that they were greatly relieved that something told them to run further tests. That is not routine procedure when a patient is already prepped for surgery. They confessed that our prayers were exactly what they had needed. One of them said that they would run one more test the next morning and that if it came back negative she would be dismissed.

Fatima awoke to see all of us rejoicing in the Lord with laughter. She mentioned a little pain and asked how the surgery had gone. Ahmad asked Javid to explain things to her.

"You explain it, Ahmad," Javid invited. "You are the one who invited us to your home to pray for her healing."

He started to give her his explanation and stopped midway

into it. "Javid, you are the one who invited Jesus the Healer into our home. You tell her what happened."

Fatima shouted with joy while Javid gave her an account of what the physicians had reported. She told us how she had prayed just before slipping into unconsciousness after they anesthetized her, "Jesus, although I have only known You for one day, let me live so that I can live for You. I know that You have healed me. You are the Healer of my life." She placed Ahmad's hand on her cheek. "Ahmed, do you want to give your heart to Jesus? Just simply Jesus?"

Ahmed looked at Javid and said, "Yes, I don't see why not!"

Javid took his hand and began to lead him in a confession of Jesus as Lord, just as his sister walked into the room. She went ballistic. She ran into the hall shrieking, "I hate you. You are nothing but an infidel and you are no longer my brother." She screamed all the way down the hallway. Fatima would not permit us to go after her.

Ahmad completed his prayer and was adopted into God's glorious family. He then began to praise the name of Jesus in Arabic. *Rabbi Yasou, ashkurak liannak khallastani min al-Islam wa-aatitani hayat abadeyya. Saazal omaggedak ela al-abad lannak shafita zawgati min marad al-saratan.* (Lord Jesus, I thank you for saving me from Islam and for giving me eternal life. I will forever give You praise for healing my wife from cancer.) At that moment Pastor Soodmand's old saying drifted from my spirit. "The angels dance in heaven when a Muslim confesses the name of Christ."

What a day that was. "Praised be Your name, Lord. That was a victorious day for Your Kingdom. In a single day You gave two lost, fanatical Muslims the gift of eternal life. You demonstrated Your healing power before Inova Hospital's brightest surgeons. You are truly awesome."

INCREASE BEGETS INCREASES

Ahmad hugged the physician the following day when he said that Fatima was cancer free and could go home. He has never returned to the mosque and has never uttered the name of Allah since. At this writing Fatima is in perfect health. Unfortunately, Ahmad's sister never had a change of heart. She followed through with her vow to disown Ahmad and his family and died after an eight-month struggle with breast cancer.

Ahmad and Fatima have become strong witnesses for the Lord within the area's Muslim community. Thursday of the week after her miracle they invited us to hold a prayer meeting in their home for some of their Muslim friends. The house overflowed with people and I took a seat on the floor with some of the others. The couple gave their respective testimonies of their conversions and about the impact that Fatima's healing had upon their lives. Thirty-five Muslims were converted that night. During the refreshment break, while I was talking with a Muslim woman, an excruciating pain shot through my right leg. It startled me so that I could hardly remain standing and she asked if I was OK.

This was a direct Satanic assault. It was his counterattack for our victories through *Touch of Christ Ministries* that were rescuing people from his grip. The enemy of our souls and bodies was very disturbed that impressive numbers of Muslims were being saved from hell and healed from the physical afflictions that he had put upon them. Undoubtedly, he was nervous about the fact that *Don't Keep Me Silent* was being distributed throughout America. All the way home that night the pain in my leg continued to intensify. I did my best to ignore it. I did not want anything to keep me from the scheduled Sunday baptismal service for Ahmad, Fatima and four other new converts. I am always deeply touched as each candidate for baptism testifies about the power of his salvation experience. It is perpetually gratifying to envision their old Islamic chains sinking behind them in the water as they arise from their baptisms.

CRUMBLING WALLS OF DECEPTION

It must be said that often we have to struggle against the devices that the devil uses in attempts to entice born-again

Muslims back into his Islamic web. At times he uses peer pressure. Middle Eastern people have extremely strong family ties. It is sometimes more than they can bear when their loved ones shun them. The deceptions of the Koran also play a part in drawing them back. By the time Muslims reach adulthood they have uttered Koranic phrases numbering in the hundreds of thousands. Each utterance puts another brick on the wall of deception that is being erected around their hearts. Salvation through Christ batters down a section of such walls. However, it essential that every Muslim convert follow through with baptism in water, baptism in the Holy Spirit and systematic Scripture memorization to complete the demolition. For these reasons a great deal of my and Javid's time is spent in spiritual warfare to ensure that each born-again Muslim remains steadfast to our Lord.

BLACK PLAGUE

Ahmad's and Fatima's baptisms went beautifully that Sunday. Each person radiated the glory of God as they came up smiling from the waters. I enjoyed every moment of the service, but was considerably distracted by the pain in my leg. Except for the bout that I had with the infection after the miscarriage, I had enjoyed perfect health. Therefore, due to that and the prospects of incurring additional medical expenses, it was not easy for me to make the decision to consult a physician about my leg. The doctor whom I decided to consult had been a missionary to Africa, and I assumed that I was in good hands on the day of my visit. I soon learned that even ex-missionaries are capable of making terrible mistakes.

I am severely allergic to any medication containing aspirin. The doctor was aware of this, but accidentally prescribed a medication that contained the dreaded substance. He administered two tablets in the office and instructed me to take one tablet every four hours until the prescription was exhausted. That night the pain did not diminish, it intensified. I dreamed that two ugly hands were gripping my leg. I awoke when I heard a chilling voice say, "Now, I have finally gotten you." My body felt like it weighed thousands of pounds and I was struggling for each breath. I was horrified when I examined myself. My leg and hands were swollen and blackened with strange bruises. I quickly examined the prescription bottle's label. To my dismay, one of the ingredients listed was aspirin.

Javid rushed me to the doctor and he directed us to go to the emergency room immediately. The whole matter of my leg was complicated by the fact that we had to carry our nine-month-old daughter everywhere that we went. The medical team at Holy Cross Hospital initially thought that I had been in an automobile accident. Their examination confirmed that I was suffering from anaphylactic allergic shock. The pills that my doctor had prescribed were poisoning my body. They were mystified by the bruises and could find no medical explanation for them. My hospital stay lasted two days and they sent me home in a wheelchair.

STANDING ON THE WORD

I became a wheelchair evangelist for the next year. I passed out tracts, conducted Bible studies and learned to diaper my baby while sitting in the wheelchair. I was not about to let this insidious attack of Satan hinder our work for the Lord. The pains, swelling and bruises did not abate. Javid pushed my wheelchair into many doctors' offices while either he or I held our infant. The medical bills amassed far beyond the level of our resources. A famous specialist put me on steroids, which caused my condition to worsen. My leg turned completely black. We reported this to him and he prescribed chemotherapy.

I asked, "Isn't that used for cancer patients?"

"Yes," he answered, "but in some cases when nothing else works we use it for conditions that are an enigma for us." I could not tolerate the possibility that I would lose my hair through that doctor's experimental option. Javid and I were both indignant in our refusal for me to undergo chemotherapy. As we left the renowned specialist's office we heard his voice trailing behind us, "You risk complete paralysis if you don't heed my advice."

MY SPECIALIST

For the next 21 days Javid and I entered an intense period of spiritual warfare and prayers for my restoration to health. I spent hours each day confessing the Bible's healing verses. Javid would join me in beseeching the Lord for my healing during any free moment that he could manage from his busy pastoral schedule. Selected members of our loving spiritual family also interceded for me. We were hesitant to let immature believers know about the seriousness of my condition, as it might hinder their faith. We rebuked Satan so many times that he must have been bruised worse than me. He really took a bruising when I discarded the wheelchair and all medications. In faith I stood to my feet and proclaimed that I had been healed by the stripes of Jesus 2,000 years ago.

Little by little, the swelling went down and the bruises faded. I progressed from painful hobbling to pain-free walking over the next 21 days. Everyone shouted with joyful praises when I walked into the church every whit whole. Some who did not know that we were praying for my healing inquired about the name of the last doctor that I visited. They incorrectly presumed that medical science could be accredited for my restoration to health.

My response was the same with each inquirer: "He is the most qualified and successful physician that the world has ever known. He is a specialist in everything. His name is Dr. Jesus Christ of Nazareth. You will find His prescription bottle in His Word, just as I did."

Satan paid a permanent price for putting that affliction upon me. We learned lessons that built our faith and enabled us to equip thousands of others with the power to quench his onslaughts. In addition, we truly learned that as ambassadors for Christ's earthly government, we have the full financial backing of His heavenly Kingdom. Like every good military general, Jesus pays for whatever His troops need.

SUPPORT FROM AFAR

Shortly after my healing, an American couple that only knew us by reputation, began to send us monthly support. This was the direct result of our systematic prayers for financial abundance. We had to do something, because our vision to reach the Muslim masses in the area eclipsed our supply of funds for the work. The level of our faith for finances began to increase and we were able to pay my medical expenses and other routine bills that had accumulated. In addition, our Commander and Chief continued to supernaturally inspire His people to send us finances. We have never had to resort to any form of manipulative strategies to glean funds for the harvest.

By faith we opened more home Bible studies for the families of Afghani and Saudi converts. For security reasons, it is often unwise for such people to openly attend church immediately after their conversions. The homicide bombings of Muslim extremists should never be perceived as events restricted to the Middle East. The word began to spread as the new Christians wrote to their friends and relatives around the States. Letters requesting materials and for us to accept speaking engagements poured in. We recorded each person's name on a prayer list. We arose at 5:00 each morning to pray for each of them by name. Several reported that they had been on the brink of suicide over their misery as Muslims. They were converted while reading *Don't Keep Me Silent* and the contemplations of suicide evaporated. Many others wrote or phoned to tell us that their prayer requests had been answered. God honored our efforts, and unsolicited funds from Christians who had hearts for the Muslim world steadily increased.

INNOVATIVE TARGETING

Through much prayer and meditation in God's Word, Javid and I came to the realization that we needed to begin to target key Islamic leaders. We launched a prayer campaign calling for the salvation of imams around the globe. Subsequently, invitations began to come in for us to meet secretly with clergymen. These had a thirst that was not being quenched by Islamic rituals. Each meeting was covered with prayers about the potential that a trap would be set to end our lives. Many such leaders have been saved and secretly exalt the name of Jesus. Islam has no miraculous healings. One of the key factors that softens these leaders, hearts for the Gospel is when they hear reports that members of their congregations and families have been restored to health through prayer in the name of Jesus. Any ministry that attempts to win Muslims without the miracle-working power of God is doomed to be ineffective.

One notable testimony came in from a famous clergyman in Iran who regularly appears on news broadcasts there and occasionally here in the States. He has every appearance of being no different than other imams. This is far from the reality about his situation. He was baptized in the bathtub of an apartment in Tehran. He regularly attends covert meetings, just as we once did. He proclaims the name of Jesus over his nation. He has full faith that the walls of Islam will soon collapse, just as the walls of communism did in Berlin years ago. For obvious reasons his name is withheld.

Two American entertainment celebrities contacted us and wanted to know more about Christ. We told them there were many American ministries that could help them. One of them responded, "For many years I have crisscrossed this nation giving performances. Thousands have applauded my expertise. To date, no one has shown any interest in my eternal welfare. I want to hear about Jesus through you guys who know what it means to suffer for His name."

JUST FRUIT

In the year 2000 we were led to expand the sponsorship of our Farsi Bible smuggling operation for Iran. They are smuggled in through various channels who either know Jesus or are friendly with someone who does. Normally the shipments are small and the Bibles are shared between four or more new

Christians. Pages are often run off on a copier to pass around. There was one unusual shipment of thousands of Bibles loaded onto a single truck. Two Iranian customs inspectors approached the truck and one of them asked what was in the load. The born-again driver told him that it was a truckload of fruit. The driver accompanied him to the back of the truck and opened the doors for his inspection. He saw the fruit that was piled on the Bibles and reached in and grabbed one of the Bibles. Holding the forbidden treasure in his hand, he asked, "Is this the type of fruit that you are carrying?"

The driver expected that the next thing that he would feel would be a shot through his head, but he answered, "Yes."

"Then you are fine, you can pass on through to Iran."

The chief inspector asked the friendly inspector about the load. "It's fruit, just fruit," he answered. They let the truck through never suspecting that there were boxes under the fruit that would produce measureless amounts of good fruit for the Kingdom of God! It is our conviction that those inspectors were either blinded by their secret love for Christ or physically blinded from making a thorough inspection.

We came to America with practically nothing. Our faith was in God and the words of knowledge about a fruitful ministry that He promised was in store for us. God is faithful. Our ministry had been greatly blessed. Believers from all across America stood with us with prayer and support. The Lord had rescued hundreds of Muslims, since we had first arrived on America's shores. Those souls were the fruits of our partners' labors as well as our own. Although we needed their help, our primary resource for blessings was God's Word. It fills us with His wisdom and power for the work at hand.

We soon found out that we were about to receive a double blessing. I discovered that I was pregnant with twins. The enemy attempted to thwart our joy by bringing complications into my pregnancy.

Chapter 8

DEATHBED DELIVERANCE

DOUBLE BLESSING

I had just finished giving my testimony at a church in Colorado and one of its elders approached me with an astonishing word of knowledge. He took me aside and told me that the Lord had given him a three-part message for me. "You are pregnant. You are carrying twins. Matters related to the birth of the babies will become complicated and cause you extraordinary pains."

At that juncture I did not even know that I was expecting. The term "babies" was enough of a shock without the additional forebodings. Immediately upon my return home, a visit to my physician confirmed the elder's word about the pregnancy. The first five months were difficult. By the sixth month, the cashier at the supermarket remarked that I was so large that she suspected that I was carrying twins. The next prenatal examination confirmed her suspicions and the second part of the Colorado elder's word. The doctor performing the sonogram exclaimed, "I see two heads and I hear two heartbeats."

I thought I might faint. "Doctor, you must be wrong."

He chuckled, "Not so, Madam. I've been doing this for 15 years and I know my business. You are carrying twins."

As he spoke, I pondered the third part of the prophetic word that stated that there would be painful complications in the pregnancy.

Our Iranian and Arab friends did not know exactly how to respond to the idea that I was having twins, as if I had control of the matter. Our American friends encouraged us by saying that twins would be a double blessing. As prophesied the birth was difficult and in March of that year my two healthy boys were delivered via Cesarean section. One weighed seven and a half pounds and the other seven pounds. We felt blessed that the boys were home and that somehow I had been spared excessive complications. We had no idea that the ordeal was not over.

The Second day of April was a beautiful, sunny, but chilly day. My two-year-old daughter and I were traveling by cab to the Fairfax hospital where I was to receive a routine postnatal exam. She had been upset by my absence from our home during the days that I was hospitalized in recovery from the C-section. It was pleasant to hear her excitedly chattering about the present that I had promised to buy for her after my scheduled 9:30 a.m. visit. Though it was only supposed to be a 10-minute exam, I sensed apprehensiveness in my heart when I entered the door of the doctor's office. I could not imagine why I felt any fear. I was unusually tired, but otherwise felt healthy. I reasoned that perhaps I was concerned about some backlash from Satan due to the success we were having in seeing Muslims evangelized. It soon became evident that my concerns were justifiable.

THE BAD SUBSTITUTE

I became unsettled in spirit as the receptionist told me that my physician was unavailable and that another would be examining me. I explained that Dr. David had requested that I see him personally, and that I wanted to postpone the appointment until I could do so. She ignored my plea and ushered me in to see his substitute. The doctor appeared with my file in hand. While he examined me, it became obvious that he was more interested in his personal affairs than he was with my health. He incessantly spoke by cell-phone to someone about his new car until I firmly asked him to get off of it.

"Look, your call is not an emergency and it makes me nervous that I do not have your full attention. Please end the call until you have completed my exam."

He offered an apology and hung up. He said that there was evidence of infection and some internal bleeding beneath the C-section's incision. I told him that Dr. David had said that a little bleeding was routine after such procedures and that I was feeling quite well. I didn't know what to say when he said that he wanted to take about 10 minutes to examine the depth of the infection. It was his plan to reopen the incision and let the infection drain. I insisted that he call Dr. David before proceeding. They wheeled me into the surgical unit and he promised to call my doctor before going ahead. It was my terrible mistake to allow him to go ahead with the procedure.

The moment his scalpel penetrated my skin, blood and puss spurted like a geyser from the wound. It was horrifying to see it splashing all over my body and the surrounding medical equipment. I could also feel the deadly fluids gushing into other parts of my abdominal cavity and my body was ablaze with heat. The intensity of the spurting showed no signs of sub siding and panic filled his face. I was covered with my own blood and cried in fright realizing he was incompetent to handle my emergency. I knew in my heart that I should have obeyed the inclination to wait for my own physician. I had fallen into Satan's murderous trap that was intended to rob me of life. He would stop at nothing in attempting to prevent Muslims from seeing the truth.

DR. "INCOMPETENT"

Dr. "Incompetent" repeatedly apologized as he told me that I would have to be admitted into the hospital. "I'm sorry, I had no idea that things would get out of hand. There is not much that I can do for you now."

My anger and fright rendered me incapable of speaking to him in a sweet little Christian tone. "You're sorry? When I repeatedly asked if you were doing the right thing, you assured me that you were. I came to this hospital feeling fine and now look at me. I can't believe that you just say, 'I'm sorry.' My two-year-old daughter is screaming from fright as she watches my life ooze from me. My husband is at home taking time from his busy schedule to care for our twins during what was supposed to be a short, routine visit to my doctor. Your apologies are insufficient for the situation that you have created."

His only response was more apologies. He sweated and scurried off with the appearance that he really knew what he was doing. It was clear that he did not have the gumption to stay and answer my questions. The attending nurse was not helpful. "It was a big mistake on your part to let that particular doctor touch you. Why on earth couldn't you wait for your own doctor?"

I didn't answer her. I was too preoccupied with thoughts about my twins, the ministry and my daughter's pleas to take her home. I could hear the voice of Dr. "Incompetent" paging another physician to report to the surgical unit for an emergency.

He reappeared and suggested that I call Javid to fetch our daughter, as I would be confined to the hospital until my condition stabilized. It was not easy to make that call as I lay there bleeding with my daughter at my side wailing for attention. It was a nightmare that eclipsed our escape from Iran, the miscarriage, my kidnapping and my bout with partial paralysis in 1999. I stammered to the nurse that I could not remember our phone number. She made the call for me and I tearfully told Javid what was happening. While I spoke with him the nurse continued to swab the blood and puss from the wound. Two other doctors and their supervisor had come on the scene and my tone with Javid increased in urgency. The last thing I heard from him was, "I'm on my way." There was a click and the phone dial-tone sounded in my ears.

OBEY THE LORD'S NUDGES

Javid rushed to my side with a faithful fellow pastor accompanying him. The pastor kindly prayed for me and assured me that his wife and another sister would give my children loving care. My little girl's fingers slipped from my hand as he picked her up to carry her from the room. Javid was faith-filled as I lay there bleeding. I overflowed with another round of tears while he began to speak.

"Mina, this is another Satanic attack. He cannot bear the thought of your continuing to bombard his kingdom by evangelizing the lost. The Lord will deliver us from this cruel attack, just as He has so many times before."

Theologically, I understood that Christians learn more about grace through hardships. I could not help but to think that I would have much preferred another teaching method at that time. I was simply unprepared for another round of hardships just as we were beginning to really enjoy the fruits of our labors for the Lord.

I was transferred to another room. A team of physicians and their supervisor surrounded my bed as they offered their opinions about the problems that confronted us. It was obvious that they were equally concerned about two interrelated issues: my condition and the fact that the hospital was liable for a malpractice suit. The major problem was that they did not know the reason for my continuing blood loss or how to stop it. Each molecule of blood that passed from my womb and into my blood stream carried deadly toxins from the infection.

At around 5:30 p.m. I heard a familiar voice echoing from down the hallway. It was my personal physician barking reprimands at the attendants who had been present when the errant doctor reopened my incision without his permission. He came into my room to console me.

"I'm so very sorry for what he has done to you. Didn't I tell you to see me personally for the checkup?" When I told him that the other doctor had promised to consult him before doing the procedure, his face became even more flushed with anger. "I never heard a word from that guy." He stomped out of the room seeking Dr. "Incompetent."

Over the next two hours he and his team tried their best to stop the bleeding through the use of various medications and antibiotics. Nothing helped. I thought that Javid might faint when his knees wobbled while Dr. David told us that I was to be taken into emergency surgery. We both felt helpless. We had babies at home and a thriving ministry that needed our attention and there we were in a crisis that was beyond our control. At that moment we both tasted what our parents must have experienced when we had to flee Iran for reasons beyond their control. Our only hope was faith that God is always in control.

DEATH'S DOOR

While we waited for the gurney to arrive that would wheel me into surgery, we prayed and repented. I confessed my failure to obey my heart when I had misgivings about going to the hospital that morning. Javid agreed with my assessment. "We both know that if we don't have peace about something, we shouldn't do it at all. Disobedience to the Lord's little nudges leads to His will being missed and can temporarily blur His glory. However, it's too late now. We will simply have to lean on His infinite mercies."

He repeated the name of Jesus over me and prayed that the Lord would overshadow all that would transpire when I was under the anesthesia. The doctor heard us praying in Farsi and inquired about our nationality. We explained that we were Christian Iranians knowing that he would presume that we were Muslims if we only stated that we came form Iran. Javid continued holding my hand in prayer while the attendants wheeled me into the operating room. He passed from my field of vision as the doors closed. I could hear his voice following me. "Be strong in the Lord. Our team of intercessors will be praying for you and He will see you through this ordeal." To me, the operating room was cold and seemed like an icy den of death. I really sensed that I was going to have a confrontation with the spirit of death.

Dr. David again apologized for the mistake. I explained to him that I had not seen my family in Iran for 18 years and did not want to die on the table without seeing them again. "I don't know what this surgery is all about. Please see that all concerned do their best to see to it that I survive." He gave me additional time to pray before signaling the anesthesiologist to put me under.

"God, I cry out to You. I'm willing to learn the lesson that You are teaching me, but please don't let Satan take my life. I claim the power of the blood of Jesus for victory over every device of the devil." I stared at the ceiling's surgical lamps and slipped into unconsciousness while saying the name of Jesus.

VIEW FROM ABOVE

Two hours later I was in the recovery room and I had a very unusual experience. It was as though I was viewing myself from above. I was lying in a pool of my own blood, was freezing cold and in great pain. I couldn't move my head and I felt strangely wet. The various tubes that were stuck into my neck and arms had the appearance of shackles that rendered my body unmovable. I could hear and see those who were speaking about me.

"Javid, your wife is passing into the valley of the shadow of death. We are helpless at this stage to do any more for her. Pain-quencher and sedative medications are being pumped into her body intravenously. We are going to leave the incision un-bandaged, exposing it to the open air to see if that helps. We advise you to call the family and your attorney." I could see the nurse changing the blood-wetted sheets, but I did not feel their dryness. The scent of my own blood filling my nostrils was disturbing. The medications proved powerless to diminish the pain, but they did help calm me down.

In the midst of all of this my spirit reasoned within me, "You are in a great battle with the enemy of every Christian's soul, the devil. He wants you to perceive this hospital room as your mortuary. Neither you, nor Javid, are to give in to him. Neither is either of you to question God's goodness. The Lord has not brought you through all of your trials only to let you be murdered by the Evil One in a Virginia hospital. Your blood loss will be quenched and you will come forth victorious."

In the wee hours of the next morning I was transferred to the Intensive Care Unit. There were twenty people assigned to my case. A medical professor from John Hopkins University Hospital headed up the team. He told us that my bleeding was a unique variety that he had not witnessed since 1976. Dr. David was a caring and sensitive Harvard graduate. He would come in and check on me four to five times daily. My blood-stained beddings were changed about once an hour. They increased the dosage of morphine in an attempt to reduce the pain. I could only bear lying on my back due to the extreme burning soreness around the open incision area. Any movement caused my whole body to ache. If I needed to shift a limb or my position I had to ask one of the attending nurses to help me. Javid was the only person who was allowed in for visits. He slept in the chair beside my bed. Speaking with him was a struggle and I could only periodically emit a few words.

THE MOCKER

The second day the bleeding had become worse. The professor asked how I was doing. "I'm tired of bleeding and the soreness, but I know that Jesus will heal me."

He scornfully smirked and chuckled gleefully as he annunciated each word. "Excuse me! Don't tell me you are one of those Jesus freaks who believe in divine healing and that God raises people from the dead."

"I wasn't always a Christian," I told him. "I was born a Muslim and after my salvation I was healed numerous times. I have seen many people receive healing from the Man who has the most notable medical practice that the world has ever known, Jesus."

"Then why are you taking up space in the ICU? If your God is such a great healer, why are you bleeding to death? Why doesn't He heal you now?"

"Sir, I wasn't bleeding when I came to this hospital. I was a woman in good health that had just given birth to a set of healthy twins. It was one of your medical experts who caused this trauma."

He insisted on taunting me with his position again, "No matter, if Jesus really heals it would seem that you would at least be showing a little improvement. I have practiced medicine in America for 32 years and have yet to see one concrete example of divine healing. I simply do not see any reasons for me to believe as you do."

Surprisingly, my speech about the Lord was a balm for my pain. Whenever I mentioned His name the pain momentarily subsided. I therefore gave him the quick version of my testimony.

He could not stand hearing the name of Jesus and stopped laughing. He impatiently made a funny face at me and asked me stop the talk about Jesus and to get some rest. I trusted Dr. David who had highly recommended this guy's expertise. I made a decision that shocked the medical team. I knew that the professor's views and attitudes would not be conducive to my restoration to health. I fired him on the spot. I told him to put down my file and to leave without bothering to return. I might have been gravely ill, but that did not stop me from discerning that he had a religious spirit of mockery and anger residing within him. I was not about to let him make another drive from Baltimore to degrade all that I valued.

He didn't believe that he was hearing me correctly and tried to act cheerfully accommodating. He made a feigned apology by saying that he had only been kidding me in order to cheer me up.

"I don't need a doctor who mocks my faith to cheer me up," I responded. "Your attitude does just the opposite. I respect your medical credentials, and you might be the only doctor around who has the scientific expertise to stop my bleeding, but I do not want you as my specialist. I have the Chief of all specialists on my case. He is my Healer and Encourager." I again ordered him from my room.

Later that day Javid noticed some large-eggplant colored sores on my back. They were swollen in a disfigured manner. He alerted the nurse about them and she said that normally such marks could be identified as bedsores. She doubted that it was the case with me due to the fact that I had not been lying in the same position long enough for them to develop. They are caused by a lack of exercise and prolonged confinement to bed. I found the smell of food revolting and refused my tray. The nurse gave me as many fluids as I could handle to quench my ever-present thirst.

On the third day, Dr. David came in with some legal papers for me to sign. He urged us to begin litigation against the hospital and the doctor who had reopened the incision. He said that we had an undeniable case for pain and suffering and that he would verify the culpability of all concerned. He frankly told us that he was confident that we would be awarded a large settlement in punitive damages for Dr. "Incompetent's" irresponsible conduct. Though we knew that we had justifiable grounds to bring a malpractice suit, we declined to do so.

A NEW MISSION FIELD

I lost track of time in the ICU and asked a nurse how long I had been there. "This is your eighth day," she answered. For me, those eight days had seemed like months. I was tired of being poked with needles and sleeping on my back. I was weary of the chill that went through me every time I heard the helicopter landing with fresh supplies of blood for me. It was disconcerting to know that their efforts to keep me alive were depleting the entire hospital's blood supply. However, I was like the woman with the issue of blood in the Bible. All of her attempts to receive healing through physicians made her worse rather than better. She was not made whole until she touched the hem of Jesus' garment. I began to imitate her faith on the eighth day. It was by far the worse day, and what I needed was just one touch from the hem of his garment. I knew that it was all I needed to go home to my husband and three small children, home to the ministry and church that I loved.

Javid was stalwart in his loving support for me the whole time of my confinement. Anytime that he could get a free moment he was by my side with words of faith and prayer. His enthusiasm for the healing power of the Lord was not in the least bit dampened by the fact that my healing was not yet apparent. The rooms of the patients adjacent to mine became his mission field. We prayed for them to be healed and led some of them to the Lord. He passed out over 70 copies of *Don't Keep Me Silent* to patients and members of the hospital staff.

When Javid came into the room on that eighth day he sensed that it was my roughest day. He tenderly took my hand while I wept and explained the many reasons that I had finally come to the end of my rope: "Javid, I can't take any more. My life is ebbing away, moment by moment, through this mysterious blood loss. My back is purple with sores and its swelling makes me look like a deformed woman, not to speak of the agonizing aches. With all of these needles in me I feel like a human pincushion. I miss my children and our friends and I can't bear the thought that you are burdened with the entire load of our ministry. Please open the window, I need a whiff of fresh air that doesn't smell like a hospital."

"Mina, everyone at the church wants to come and lay hands on you for healing," he told me. "You know that they would be here in a moment if the doctors would allow it. Your name is on their lips day and night as they intercede on your behalf, and God will answer their prayers. My dear, I promise that Jesus will not fail to raise you from this bed of affliction." He then offered a powerful prayer for me that was interspersed with the name of Jesus and quotes from the Word of God. He sat with me for hours and then left for the evening.

HEALING COMFORTER

His departure brought a new round of weeping. It was dark and I was again alone in that miserable bed with those intolerable pains. The tears trickled down the side of my face and wetted my pillow. I cried out a prayer that seemed to be my millionth: "Lord Jesus, God have mercy on me. It is me, Your child. I'm begging You for healing and relief. All that I need is just one touch of Your healing hand on my incision and I will again be able to serve You. Touch my heart with a greater impartation of faith for my healing. You are my Creator and my life is Yours. Touch my life for Your glory. Lord, stop this flow of blood in the name of Jesus." I fell asleep with that prayer, but was gloriously awakened in the early morning hours of the ninth day.

I rubbed my eyes to make sure that I was not dreaming. A tall figure stood glowing with heavenly glory in the corner of my room. Every molecule in the room was glistening with the Shekinah presence of the Holy Spirit. I cried out to the Lord and I heard His familiar voice coming to me from the corner of the room. It was Jesus, the Son of God.

"Lift up your hands!"

I complained that I couldn't and the voice boomed forth again. "Lift up your hands!"

Miraculously, I lifted them up from the restraints of the intravenous entrapments that bound me. The moment that I did so I saw beams of light continuously bouncing from one of Jesus' hands to the other. Suddenly my two hands were added to the process. His hands and mine were like the four corners of a rectangle with the radiant beams of healing light connecting them.

"Mina, your bleeding has stopped and you will live." The voice spoke with such authority that I knew that my bleeding was over. I looked at my sheet and bed cloths and they were dry and unspotted by blood.

Apparently, one of the nurses saw me lifting my hands and heard me talking to someone. The attendants rushed into the room with Dr. David close on their heels. They were all frantic that I might have undergone a mental collapse. I told them that Jesus had visited me and that He had stopped my bleeding. They looked at me with unbelief and I told them to check my bedding for blood. They found none. Dr. David naively asked them to tell him the name of the last coagulant medication that had been administered to me. He assumed that they had finally found a medication that worked. I reiterated that Jesus had come and healed me and pointed to the spot where He had stood in the corner. A thorough exam proved that the bleeding had indeed come to an end and they transferred me from ICU into a regular room. One of the nurses called my home to give my family the news, and Javid rushed over. He was overjoyed and told me that the saints had interceded for me at the church throughout the night. No one could deny that God had answered our prayers.

DEVASTATING NEWS

Visitors from my spiritual family began to flood into my room. They all wanted to hear the account of my visitation from the Lord. They were welcomed, but I was still weak from my ordeal. At times, when another group came in, all I could manage was a smile before slipping off into a slumber. The trauma of the sickness had somewhat blurred my cognitive processes. At times, I had difficulty remembering the names of friends and just who had come and gone from the room.

The cessation of the blood flow was not the end of my battle with Satan. He had other tricks up his sleeve. Several days after the first installment of my healing, Javid was examining my back and called the doctor in alarm. They were both disturbed that my skin looked worse. The doctor initiated another round of various antibiotics and sent me in for an MRI. The results were devastating. The image of my liver revealed that it was greatly damaged and that a liver-transplant was required. Apparently, the swelling and eggplant coloration on my back was partially due to my problematic liver. In addition, the incision was still open and I was running a high fever.

Soon after the MRI, a new surgeon came into the room and introduced himself as Dr. Thompson. He cheerfully informed me that a new liver had become available for me and that he wanted to take me to surgery as soon as possible. Javid responded in a manner that was uncustomary for him. He marched toward the surgeon and told him that he could give the liver to someone else. "My wife will not endure another scalpel being inserted into her body. This is another assault of Satan and we will not accept it. Please leave the room."

While that doctor was in the process of exiting, Dr. David came in and told us the reasons that the surgery was a necessity. Again, the hospital was at fault. During all of their frantic efforts to help me in the ICU, they had accidentally administered medications that counteract one another and cause liver damage. He, of course, explained that he was very sorry for yet another medical blunder.

"Sure you're sorry!" I exploded. "Are you telling me that I have to undergo another surgery due to this hospital's mistakes? Are you sure that you really know what you are talking about? We both know that there is a chance that my body will not accept the new liver."

Poor Dr. David tried to explain that we had no choice in the matter and Javid interrupted him. "Oh, but we do have a choice. We choose to ask Jesus to give her a new liver without any surgery."

The doctor left the room mystified by our refusal. Javid also departed. He was going to a special gathering at a church in Washington, D.C. that was known for the power of the Holy Spirit. He knew that it would be filled with friends and fellow ministers who would fervently agree with him in prayer about my situation.

RED FLAG

While he was there, a revelation from the Holy Spirit came into his heart. He felt that the Lord was telling him that the time was ripe to take final authority over Satan. He was led to do something that was rather unusual. The church had flags of various colors that were waved as the congregants glorified the Lord. He ripped a red one from its staff. He wrapped it around his Bible and placed it upon the location of his liver and prayed for me in proxy.

"In the name of Jesus, I cast every demonic power of infirmity from Mina. She is going to live and not die. She will proclaim the goodness of God in the land of the living. Satan, I command you and all of your minions out of her hospital room." He then left the meeting with the assurance of victory in his heart and returned to my side.

It was 10:30 p.m. when he walked into the room, and the nurse had just remarked that I was running a high fever. Without saying a word he tossed the cloth from the red flag over my abdomen. What happened next was like a scene from the Book of Acts. Everything in the room that was not attached to the floor, including me, began to shake under the power of the Holy Spirit. Food trays rattled and glasses of water spilled over. Javid and the nurse were also visibly trembling. The manifestations abated just as quickly as they had appeared. The nurse regained her composure and retook my temperature. Hallelujah! It was normal.

A beloved sister in the Lord, who was a gifted doctor, was called in as a consultant to the medical team about my liver. The Holy Spirit guided her with innovations that normalized it. Dr. David came in with news of another exciting miracle. My liver was as healthy as a newborn's and no surgery was required. He was beside himself with joy over my remarkable recovery from death's door. The only thing that prevented me from being dismissed from the hospital was that my incision had not yet healed.

On the 24th of April they decided to begin stitching it from the inside out. Their plan was to work in stages stitching each level as the previously stitched levels showed improvement. The local anesthetics that they used were to no avail. The stitching process was excruciating. I screamed and thrashed my legs in agony. The chief surgeon was on the floor and ran to the room to see what they were doing to me. Each layer of new stitches put me through the same degree of pain. I could not help shuddering with fright each time they came in for a new application of stitches.

ANOTHER EXPERT

Due to my weakness and weight loss they continued to give me hemoglobin. A hematologist was called in and his diagnosis was that I had an internal bleeding disorder. He wanted to examine my entrails through an endoscope to verify his suspicions. He warned us that the shunt would have to remain in me for quite a while. He urged us to give him a prompt response when we told him that we would have to pray about it. I had been hospitalized for almost a month and we did not look forward to another procedure that could be hit-or-miss for my health.

Several days later the hematologist was still waiting for our decision and I really did not want to keep him waiting any longer. While I was pondering what to say, an East Indian nurse came to me and said that I needed to call home. Like all mothers, my first thought was that something was amiss with one of the children. At 9:00 p.m. on April the 27th, Javid excitedly spoke words of faith, "Mina, the Lord has spoken to me that tomorrow is the day of your complete healing. You will walk out of that hospital on your own accord tomorrow."

I rejoiced in his words and fell asleep with my Bible in my hand. I had been reading and praying through the Psalms and seeking the Lord for guidance while awaiting Javid's arrival the next day. During the night the Lord gave me a spiritual vision. It was an open vision like the prophet Ezekiel had when he was translated bodily to the temple. My body felt like it was soaring somewhere. I saw myself dressed in my hospital gown lying in a lush garden and all of the I-V tubes were hanging from my body.

Suddenly, I heard a voice speaking from behind the foliage and saw the face of a holy angel peering at me: "Mina, Mina, stand up. You are healed. Go home." To my amazement I opened my eyes and found that I was standing in the hospital's lobby. No one had wheeled me there in a wheelchair. God had transported me there in the vision. The medical attendants began to scurry around asking one another how I had gotten there. The doctors quizzed me, "Who brought you here?" I was so elated that all I could say was, "I don't really know. I just know that I'm going home." They wheeled me back to my room and put me to bed.

YES, I HEARD GOD

The next day the doctor's response was as expected. "You can't just leave. You're still an ill woman who possibly has internal bleeding. You could bleed to death if you go home." Dr. David came and sat on my bed and tried to reason with me. I told him about the vision that had delivered me to the lobby, and what the angel had said to me. He did not attempt to deny what I reported.

After a lot of discussion he asked, "Mina, do you really think that an angel told you that you are healed?"

I confidently said, "Yes."

"Mina, I know that you think that you are well, but you're not. The entire medical team believes that you are dying. We don't know what the problem is and we really need to run more batteries of tests. Do you still want to go home?"

Again my answer was, "Yes." He pleaded for me to stay just a few more days for a few more tests. He assured us that if everything proved all right he would sign my discharge papers. We would have none of it, because we knew that the Lord's command was that I go home. He finally acquiesced to our desires and signed my discharge papers. The other doctors would not even touch it. I informed them that one way or the other I was leaving.

"If you don't let me go I will yank out these I-Vs and walk out." They all plainly saw that they no longer had any options but to comply with our request.

On that 27th day of April, the nurses unplugged all of the medical devices under Dr. David's supervision. I took off my gown and dressed myself in street clothes. All of the floor's medical staff applauded as Javid and I walked triumphantly to the elevator. Dr. David humbly approached me with tearful eyes for some parting words: "Mina, when you came out of that surgery room, none of the experts thought that you would live more than a few days. Today you are walking out. I have seen what can only be described as miracles occurring in your life. The bleeding stopped. Your liver is perfect. And you somehow got down into the lobby that night when you couldn't even walk. You know, I have never said these kinds of things to anyone. You guys are really people of God. Would you please remember me in your prayers?" While he embraced me, I assured him that he would be in our prayers, and gave him a copy of my book. He promised that he would read it.

CHAIN OF MIRACLES

In obedience to the Lord, Javid did not assist me as we walked out into the fresh, invigorating air. The Lord had raised me from what the devil surely intended to be my deathbed. I lifted my hands in praise to the Lord and Javid took his Bible and loudly read Isaiah 53:5 - *But He was wounded for our transgressions, He was bruised for our iniquities; The chastisement for our peace was upon Him, And by His stripes we are healed.*

Three more miracles occurred. The first happened while we were getting into the car in the parking lot. One of the Muslim nurses, whom Javid had spoken to about Jesus, ran out to meet us. She said that she had read my book, heard about my healing and wanted to give her heart to the Lord. Right beside the car she was gloriously converted.

The second was that the hospital sent us a bill for absolutely zero. My hospitalization and all the tests amounted to over one half of a million dollars. The bill they sent us is cited at the end of this chapter. It's a lot like Calvary. Jesus did not simply forgive our sins, He completely remitted them. He cast them into the sea of God's forgetfulness as though they never existed. That is what happened to our debt to the hospital.

After my discharge I never took another single pill and never returned for checkups. God healed me perfectly, and I was healthier than ever. Jesus brought me back to my home walking on my own two feet through three magnificent miracles. My first Sunday back in church I gave my testimony and two powerful men of God dedicated our twins to the Lord. After hearing my testimony, four Muslims came forward and gave their hearts to Christ. The third miracle was the salvation of Dr. David.

Seven months after my discharge I got a surprise phone call from him and he gave me his astounding testimony: "After your dismissal I read *Don't Keep Me Silent* several times and was deeply touched by it. A battle with my intellect raged within me. However, I considered the miracles that I had witnessed during your hospitalization and suddenly I began to see God in everything around me.

"While on vacation in Hawaii, I made the acquaintance of a clergyman who was sitting next to me at the hotel's bar. I told him all about you, and he was very impressed. On the way back to our rooms I discovered that he just happened to be occupying the room across the hall from me. About 2:00 a.m. I started reviewing your book and reading the Bible that I had brought along. I heard Someone telling me to go and knock on the minister's door. It sounded like the same voice that you had described hearing in your experiences. My analytical mind told me that I was going berserk, but I obeyed the voice.

"Before I could even knock, he opened the door and kindly inquired, 'What do you want my son?'

"'You know why I am here.' He invited me in and I knelt down by his bed. I told him that I wanted to give my heart to that same Jesus who healed the Iranian lady whom I had told him about. He led me in a prayer of repentance for my sins and a confession of Christ. I confessed that I feared that my medical expertise would cause me to try to rationalize away my experience in the morning. I asked if he would mind baptizing me in the hotel's swimming pool the first thing the next morning.

"At 6:00 a.m. I arose from the chlorine waters of that pool, a new creation in Jesus. Previously, I was an accomplished physician who acted like he thought he had the world by the tail.

Inwardly, it was a bluff. I always knew that something was missing from my life. Today I have that 'something.' I would not trade it for all of the world's riches and claims to fame. Now, I am your brother in Christ. I've got everything plus Jesus."

At Christmas he sent me a beautiful floral arrangement. The attached card thanked me for introducing him to our miracle-working God. My brush with death was worth every drop of blood that I lost and every pain that I endured. Seventy of my books were distributed among the staff, and a number of them accepted the Lord. Some were saved from the perils of Islam. Three marvelous examples of God's wonder-working power were demonstrated before the eyes of some of Virginia's most renowned physicians. At least one of them had come to the Lord. What could be better than that? My response was to renew the vow to my King that I had made the night of my escape from the Muslim kidnappers in Amsterdam. I again vowed to serve Him faithfully, no matter what the costs, as long as there was breath in my body.

INPATIENT STATEMENT OF ACCOUNT   **INOVA FAIRFAX HOSPITAL**

PATIENT NAME	ACCOUNT NO.	ADMISSION DATE	DISCHARGE DATE	STATEMENT DATE
NEVISA, MINA		04/02/01	04/27/01	05/02/01

PLEASE REFER TO PATIENT'S NAME AND ACCOUNT NO. ON ALL INQUIRIES AND CORRESPONDENCE

DIRECT ALL INQUIRIES TO PATIENT ACCTS'   PHONE 703 764-2801

BILL TO:	REMIT TO:
MINA NEVISA	INOVA FAIRFAX HOSPITAL P.O. BOX 16013 FALLS CHURCH, VA 22040-1613

MAKE CHECKS PAYABLE TO ABOVE INSTITUTION

FOR BILLING INFORMATION CALL   703 645-2899

MEDICAID VA   W92

VISA *MasterCard*   (See reverse side if credit card payment is desired)

IMPORTANT: PLEASE DETACH AND RETURN THE TOP PORTION OF THIS STATEMENT WITH YOUR REMITTANCE TO ASSURE PROPER CREDIT.

PATIENT NAME	ACCOUNT NO.	STATEMENT DATE	PAGE NO	
NEVISA, MINA		05/02/01	SM02	THE INSURANCE PORTION IS COMPUTED ACCORDING TO THE INFORMATION SUPPLIED BY YOUR INSURANCE CARRIER.

DATE	REF. NO.	DESCRIPTION	TOTAL AMOUNT	INSURANCE PORTION	PATIENT PORTION
	0730	EKG/ECG	184.50		
	0920	OTHER DIAGNOSTIC SERVICES	424.00		
	0942	EDUCATION/TRAINING	100.50		
		TOTAL OF ALL OTHER CHARGES	506,890.85		
		ESTIMATED INSURANCE AMOUNT		523,665.85	
		NOTHING DUE AT THIS TIME			

INOVA HEALTH SYSTEM

Inova Emergency Care Center   Inova C.A.T.S.   Inova Kellar Center   Inova Fairfax Hospital
Inova Fair Oaks Hospital   Inova Mount Vernon Hospital

Chapter 9

The Divine Encounter

Maturing in the Lord

Time passes so quickly. It has been almost two years since the day I crooned songs of victory when I walked into my home healed and delivered from death's door. Regardless of all the calamities that have befallen Javid and I, we know that we are in the right place at the right time. Our path is continually illuminated by the overflow of God's wonders in our lives. Our thoughts of our homeland's delightful seasons and ravishingly beautiful landscapes are sweet, but distant memories. So much has occurred that the sound of the rusty chains of Islam falling from my life as I uttered my first prayer of faith in Christ, are becoming a fainter tingle.

I am no longer the frightened, tearful teenager who fled through the mountains over twenty years ago. Our years in exile and experiences with the grace of God in the midst of adversities have matured me. The sunsets of disappointments still occasionally come, but I am hardly aware of them. They are diminished by the glory of the Son of God's sunrises in our hearts which we anticipate each day.

Our love for Muslims and commitment to see them translated from the kingdom of darkness to the Kingdom of God's light has intensified. It is such a joy to see them cease their hopes of traveling to Mecca just to fruitlessly circle the Kaaba stone. Many who once did, now join us in endless praises to the living Son of God. During an 11-month mission trip to

California, scores of souls were converted and abandoned their nightlife debaucheries. The fruit was so plentiful that we were compelled to plant two new churches. Satan still tries to send the hurricanes of life our way. We weather them victoriously and refuse to be tossed to and fro spiritually and emotionally because of them. Each day is valued as a new opportunity to learn more about the Lord's salvation truths and to patiently wait for the day that our exile will end.

To this day, we win Muslims for Christ and see many testify of healings from various chronic ailments. In addition, it remains our habit to pray for a change of heart with my family members, especially within my father. Up until recently, I never approached our mailbox without the hope of finding a letter announcing my parent's salvation in Iran. I often questioned how long it would take before someone within the family would encounter the Lord through the efforts of our prayers.

A CALL IN THE NIGHT

The children were growing older and it had been about two years since I had heard from my mother. It was difficult for me to find creative ways of answering them when they asked about their grandparents and when they would be able to meet them. I had been careful to not let them see me weeping after one of their episodes of questions.

One particular week Javid and I were fasting about the direction for the ministry and the telephone rang at 3:30 a.m. on a Saturday . Due to a powerful prayer meeting that we had on Friday evening, the children had been put to bed late. I was still up working on this book when the phone sounded. Javid was already asleep and I quickly answered it, assuming that it was likely one of the converts who had returned to Iran and was reporting in to us. They frequently call in the middle of the night.

For some momentarily unexplained reason I was shaking as I reached for the phone. No voice came through so I hung up and returned for bed when no one answered my hello. The same thing happened a second time and I decided that I would not answer it if it rang again. It shortly sounded forth for the third time and I dutifully answered it. I heard the operator speaking in Farsi stating that it was a person-to-person call for me from Iran. I assured the operator that I was the person whom the call was for and she told the other party that I was on the line. The male voice that I heard explained the reason for my shaking. Even before I picked up the receiver, the Holy Spirit within me knew who it was. The rush that His presence was causing in my body facilitated my physiological response of shaking. It was my father.

GLORIOUS SHOCK AND AWE

"Mina, my beloved daughter, is that really you?" I could not respond instantly due to the fact that I was choking with tears. It was the first time that I had heard his voice in over 20 years. Thoughts of his renunciation of me as his daughter, and yelling that my name had been eradicated from his identification papers, rushed through my mind. I wanted to speak, but the years of pain forbade his name from spilling over my lips. I rationalized within that it could not be him and was someone with a voice that sounded like his.

"Please excuse me, I must talk with Mina. Mina, Mina is that you? Please talk to me." His repetitions of my name, which he had vowed to never utter again, finally solicited my affirmation that it was I.

"Yes, this is Mina. Father, is this really you?" I wailed and slipped to the floor and he gave me the following testimony that convinced me that God had heard every prayer for him that had ever passed through my vocal chords.

HOLY GROUND ENCOUNTER

"Yes, my dearest daughter, it is I, your father. It has been so many years, and I have secretly longed to call you many times. I am especially sad that I remained silent in my stubbornness after you had the miscarriage in Turkey. If I had it to do over again I would have surely expressed my regrets for your loss of the baby earlier."

At that point, I interrupted him and choked with tears, "Father, you don't have to apologize. I love you so very much, and only God knows how much I have missed you and would love to see you again. It has been a great burden on my heart since the day that I ran away from your home. It was the worst day of my life."

"Mina, I never demanded that you flee," he said. "It was also your home." Then I heard my mothers muffled voice while she asked father to give her the phone. She wept as she called me her beloved Mina. By this time, Javid had come to my side and prayed as my father continued his story.

"My dear Mina, just listen carefully to what I want to tell you about what has happened to me in the last couple of days. Early Thursday morning I left Tehran for our farm in the country, and arrived there around noon. Even though it is not Ramadan, I decided to spend the day fasting. I was alone, as your mother was at one of our other estates. I was scheduled to return home later that evening. There were errands to run and I was tired and hungry when I got to the farm. I walked around a little and then decided to return home, only to find that I had accidentally locked the keys in the car. I did not welcome the prospect of walking all the way to town to fetch a locksmith. I opted to recite my *salat* before the cold darkness closed in and before attempting the journey.

The waters of the well were cold as I splashed them over my face, arms, loins and feet in ablution before kneeling in prayer. I was famished with hunger and as I knelt I saw a package of warm, freshly baked bread lying in the grass. There was not a soul around for miles and I began to thank Allah for His provision. I put a piece to my mouth and heard a thunderous voice telling me to arise to my feet. I obeyed and as I arose a heavy rain began to fall over me. To my astonishment, the voice commanded me to look around. It was then that I noticed that it was only raining on me and nowhere else on the farm. The ground under my feet was soaked and everywhere else the ground was perfectly dry.

"The voice came again, 'Do you know who I am? I am the Bread of Life.' My response was, *Allaho Akbar*, God is Great. 'No, you are mistaken. I am not Allah. You don't know Me at all. Kneel before Me.' When I knelt, a radiant figure appeared in front of me. The light from it was so bright that I had to lift my hands to shield my eyes.

"'You are to repent of your sins. I am the Bread of Life and today My blood washes your sins away.' I fell face-forward into the wet ground and cried out the name of Jesus repeatedly. As I did so, something that felt like a heavenly electrical honey pulsated through my entire body. I screamed into the muddy ground, '"Even though I am now an old man please accept me, Jesus, and I will serve You for the rest of my life.'

"The voice became even louder and continued, 'You are to prepare a feast of salvation at your home for all to see.' I knew that I had to rush home and tell your mother what had occurred. To my amazement, when I reached for the open package of bread, which was beside me, it and the ground that I had been lying upon were completely dry. However, my clothes were still thoroughly soaked, and I had no choice but to head for home in that condition. In my excitement, I had forgotten that the keys were locked in the car, and I put my hand on the door handle. Miraculously, it swung open and I found the keys in the ignition where I had left them.

"I explained every detail about my divine encounter to your mother. I enthusiastically announced that I now believed as you do because I had experienced the same type of visitation that you had once described. She gently reprimanded me for my previous attitudes and then hugged me as she wept for joy. 'Oh, so you now believe in Jesus like Mina?' she berated me. 'Don't you think that it is a little late seeing how you drove her from our home all those years ago? You are so strange. Because of your fanatical concerns about your precious Islam, you disowned our wonderful daughter who was carrying your grand-child. How could you do such a thing simply to protect your reputation as an Islamic scholar within this ridiculously barbarous regime of the Ayatollah's?'

"She then embraced me with deep affection. 'My husband, I'm so very proud of you. You can never imagine how I have longed and prayed for the day that I would hear you speaking as you are now. After more than twenty years, it is wonderful to hear you lovingly utter Mina's name with such high esteem. I will do everything that I can to help you prepare the grand banquet for the Lord that you have been commanded to serve in our home.'"

FORGIVENESS AND RESTORATION

In the background I could hear my mother ecstatically praising the Lord, and my father went on with the story of his conversion. Javid and I, in Washington, D.C., and my parents in Tehran, cried praises to Jesus, as each detail was recounted. That night the Lord gave my father a dream wherein he saw their estate enshrouded by the sparkling branches of a heavenly tree. One of the branches had the name of a famous Islamic politician and Iranian television celebrity, who had come to know the Lord, inscribed upon it. This man had chosen to maintain his appearance as a Muslim, knowing that it would give him the liberty to smuggle Bibles into the country and to attend secret meetings. Father sought him out, and it was he who gave him my telephone number and baptized him.

Toward the end of our conversation I asked my father whether or not he had asked the authorities to reinstate my name on his identification papers. He assured me that he had, as it was important for personal and legal reasons. On the personal level it was evidence that he truly claimed me as his daughter and would risk his reputation for Jesus. On the legal end of things it would prevent complications about his last will and testament after his death. He assured me that he had indeed officially reinstated my status. Of course, Iran's Islamic regime still hated me and would slaughter me if given the opportunity. However, it was good to know that my father had taken such a bold step for me.

"My daughter," he said, "you have always been my favorite child and now you are even more precious to me. Without a doubt, I know that everything you believe about Jesus being the divine Son of God is true, and that He dwells in each of our hearts. I really need to know, do you really forgive me for all of the heartache that I have brought to you and Javid?"

"Father, we love you with all of our hearts," I answered. "We forgave you years ago, and all of our animosities toward the Islamic authorities have been washed away by the blood of Jesus and the waters of baptism. Hundreds of Christians here in America and ex-Muslims around the world have been praying for your conversion. Because of your confession of Jesus, the angels are joining Jesus in a dance of joy. When all of our Christian friends hear the news, we know they will do the same.

Then memories of the happy years of my childhood began to flood through my heart. His big smile the day that he brought home the stroller only days after it was discovered that I was pregnant loomed into my mind. My heart leapt with the anticipation that I would not need to make any more excuses for my children not meeting their grandparents.

MIRACLE OF MIRACLES

It might be easy for readers, privileged by birth in free democracies, to underestimate the strategic spiritual dynamics of my father's call. Like Communism did, worldwide Islam is doomed to crumble. It will because our faith in Christ provides the victory that overcomes the world's evils. When Islam falls, and it will, hundreds of thousands of ex-Muslims will be liberated to evangelize their nations. My father's name carries significant weight with knowledgeable Muslims. His father was an author and a world-renowned authority on Islamic issues. My father was a professor of theology in Iran's most influential university. When those who are preaching to Muslims give his miraculous testimony, many will be convinced that Jesus is Lord. These will deduce that if he saw the Lord and spoke with Him, and was saved, salvation through Jesus' name has to be legitimate. In addition, ex-Muslim Christians are now equipped with a new enthusiasm for prayer. Any of them who hear that God answered our years of prayer for my parents will be encouraged that the same can happen to theirs. Now, I can never grow weary in intercessions for the global Islamic community. Anytime one of them is saved it is a miracle. My father's salvation was a most notable miracle of miracles.

Chapter 10

My Privileged Friends

You have completed reading the story about Jesus of Nazareth's miraculous interventions in my life from my teen years through the past 21 years. I hope that it does not shock you, but I consider you as a friend. The reason is, I have shared more about my life experiences with you than I have my parents or any of my closest schoolmates whom I knew in Iran. Therefore, my friend, I want to conclude with two sets of remarks that are especially for you. If you are already a Christian, I will share my thoughts with you in this chapter. If you happen to be Muslim, I have a special message for you at the end of this book's addendum. I urge every reader to prayerfully read through it, as it contains essential information for anyone who wants to know the truth about Islam.

YOU ARE PRIVILEGED

You have learned from reading about my life that not every Christian has the freedom to publicly express their faith like you do. Due to a lack of exposure to those who suffer for their faith in Christ, many believers in democratic societies are insensitive to the plights of their persecuted brethren. There is a Bible verse that I would like for you to ponder in your heart. It relates to people like your brethren who are living in Islamic states who have secretly converted to Christianity. Even though they may not be physically behind bars, they are nonetheless the spiritual prisoners of Islam. Every time they attend a covert meeting, open a Bible (if they even own one), or boldly share their faith with a Muslim, they risk imprisonment, torture and death. Hebrews 13:3- *Remember the prisoners as if chained with them—those who are mistreated—since you yourselves are in the body also.*

These dear souls are depending on you to pray and to fast for changes to take place in their lives and nations. Communism fell in Eastern Europe because millions of free Christians interceded for their oppressed brothers and sisters in the Lord. Most did so, in part, out of educated self-interest. They wisely perceived that Communism's goal was world domination, and at all costs they wanted to avoid its takeover of their homelands. Be assured that Islam is a far greater threat. The Koran's mandate for every Muslim is the Islamization of every nation on the planet. You cannot afford to presume that it can't happen to America and to other Christianized nations. Always remember that most of the countries found in your Bible's maps were once bastions of Christianity. They are not functioning in that manner today. By the tenth century they had all fallen under the crescent moon of Islam. Mosques now stand where churches once did in Israel, Lebanon, Jordan, Turkey, Syria, Egypt, Libya and Albania. I plead with you not to be slack in the fervency of your prayers that Islam will crumble and that thousands of Christians living in those nations will be liberated to freely preach the Gospel.

GOD'S SECRET WEAPON

Your prayers and support can unleash one of God's secret end-time weapons, Muslims who have been converted to Christ. I call them His secret weapon because they have cultivated disciplines that every Christian should have. Many western Christians struggle to pray daily, fast, memorize verses, honor the Word of God, and to be bold witnesses. Though they are misdirected, Muslims have prayed multiple times daily all of their lives. Most of them fast during the month of Ramadan. Every Islamic child is taught to recite scores of Koranic verses and the *Salat* prayers in Arabic. Keep in mind that for a majority of them, Arabic is not their mother tongue. Only 25% of the world's Muslims actually speak fluent Arabic. As an act of honor, it is rare for a Muslim to pick up or put away a Koran without kissing it. They have no problems in being bold about their faith. While many Christians are hesitant to even pray over their meals in public, Muslims spread their prayer rugs, no matter where they are, and pray five times daily.

Consider the implications for the purposes of Christ when millions of Muslims are converted to Christ. They will quickly be transformed from those who labor under illegitimate Islam into dynamic believers who are strong in authentic New Testament Christianity. All of their previous disciplines were seemingly to no avail, because they were paying homage to an inept, false deity, Allah. However, God rewards those who diligently seek Him. The reward will not come to them through Islam. Their reward will come through their conversions to Christ. Think what will happen when they apply their customary fervency to the name of Jesus and the Word of God. The results that they will derive through their prayers about their personal circumstances will cause them to become even more enthusiastic about the Lord. Like nuclear warheads, they will explode within the unsuspecting Islamic world with powerful spiritual gifts of the Spirit and productive faith. Their nations will be revolutionized from poverty to world influencing productivity.

Satan's kingdom will incur tremendous damage due to the evangelism exploits of people who have been converted from Islam. The religion of Islam is corrupt and destructive. Muslim people are a different matter. The societies in which they live existed long before Islam took over. Regardless of the perils that came through Islam, those cultures were built on strong family values and neighborly interdependence that remain to this present day. Here is where they have an innate advantage over many of their fellow believers who were born in Western nations. Unlike many Americans and Europeans, Muslims from the Middle East are generally extremely social people. They are not hindered by endless material distractions like we are. Their days are spent in close-knit neighborhoods where everyone knows everyone by name. The majority of them spend far more time conversing with their relatives, friends and business associates than most Christians do. This makes ex-Muslims extraordinary conduits for the most effective form of evangelism, friendship evangelism. Once they are armed with a faith that works they will easily witness to everyone about what they have experienced through Christ's wonder-working power. The sick will be healed, relationships will be restored and millions will renounce Muhammad's Allah.

YOUR PIVOTAL ROLE

In addition to your essential role of praying for the collapse of Islam and the salvation of the Muslim world, you have another pivotal role. It is to personally witness to Muslims and to support ministries that evangelize them. The following points will help you become an effective witness to Muslims. If you wish to learn more about witnessing to Muslims, you are welcomed to contact *Touch of Christ Ministries* at the address provided at the end of this chapter.

•   **Make sure that you have something to export** – Muslims are the captives of a false religion that offers no power and no potential for a life giving, two-way relationship with God. They don't need another religion. They need a viable relationship with God and His Son through the power of the Holy Spirit. A very wise man once said, "*If Christianity is not working for you, it is wrong to try to export it to others.*" Muslims are generally observant people who are deeply committed to their faith. They will not be easily impressed by syrupy testimonies about the love of Jesus unless there is something distinctive about the lives of those who are bearing the name of Jesus.

Most will not be interested in importing what you want to export to them unless they can see clear evidence that it has been beneficial for you. This dictates several things. You will need to embrace full faith in the name and blood of Jesus and confidence in the unfailing power of the Word of God. You must be proficient in praying for the sick and in exercising other spiritual gifts in a manner that gets results. You must have up-to-date testimonies of what God has done for your own family and circumstances.

• **Sincere friendliness** – The best way to win Muslims to Jesus is through friendship evangelism. This means that any efforts to convert them must be preceded by demonstrations that you truly value them as individuals and genuinely care for the welfare of their families. During this period it is strategic that they see that God answers your prayers and that your faith in Christ makes you a loving, hospitable, courteous and productive person. In this regard it is helpful for you to pray for their needs and those of their family while in their presence. Do not offer mini-sermons as you pray for them. Simply pray for specific needs in the name of Jesus and then follow up with inquiries about how things are going.

• **Timing is everything** – The signal that it is time to share the Gospel message is an occasion when they have seen some dramatic answer to your prayers for them. When this happens they will normally initiate questions about your faith. It is good to open with some type of gentle statement that defines why people from other nations desire to immigrate to Christianized nations. The reason being, the Christian faith nurtured the prosperity and blessings of God that make those nations attractive. Statements of this nature are posed to get Muslims pondering why Islam has not brought similar blessings to their homelands.

• **Know the differences between Islam and Christianity** – The addendum of this book will arm you with a wealth of information in this area. To continue beyond this point it is helpful to be familiar with all of the Koranic verses that speak about Jesus. This will enable you to flow from areas where Islam and Christianity are in agreement into areas where they differ. You will need to be equipped to present biblically sound, cohesive logic for your beliefs in the trinity, the divinity of Christ and His sacrificial death and physical resurrection. You should also be prepared to offer explanations for the Christian concepts of forgiveness, freedom from stringent requirements to conform to religious laws, eternal security and the assurance of heaven. All of these are absent from Islam.

• **Patience is golden** – Do not push for a single conversation to be the impetus to convert them. When Muslims are won to Jesus, it is normally the fruit of numerous relaxed and friendly conversations. Very often their conversions are facilitated by direct supernatural encounters with the Lord. Gently entreat them to ask God the Father to reveal Jesus to them by the power of the Holy Spirit

• **Get them grounded** – Give them a Bible in their native tongue. Local members of the Gideons can secure Bibles in any language for you. See to it that they are baptized in water and the Holy Spirit in a close proximity to their salvation experience. Get them into a fellowship that understands Islamic issues, preaches the Word of God and demonstrates the power of the Holy Spirit.

GREAT EXPECTATIONS

My friend, your God is expecting great fruit from your life. Remarkably, Jesus said that future generations of His unified disciples would perform even greater works than He performed during His earthly ministry (Jn. 14:12). In addition, the Bible says that much is required of those to whom much has been given (Lk. 12:48). The implications are that God has yoked you with a significant degree of responsibility to see that those who have not enjoyed the same abundances come to the saving light of Jesus Christ. The global Muslim community falls within the realms of your responsibilities. Though it may be difficult to fathom, you have been graced with world-transforming authority through the name of Jesus and the power of the Holy Spirit.

Your residence in a free country is no accident. God specifically planted you where you are for His divine purposes. He wants you to cultivate a vision beyond getting your own needs met. It is His expectation that you will use all of the wonderful spiritual tools at your disposal to become a vibrant witness for Him. To accomplish this you will have to embrace the Christian disciplines of prayer and fasting that I have spoken of in this chapter. Be specific in your prayers and continue them in faith until you see the breakthroughs that you are seeking.

Through faith, patience and endurance you will be able to present a beautiful harvest to your King. He has also blessed you with the strength to be productive in your vocation so that you will have the abundance for every good work (2 Cor. 9:8). Our ministry to Muslims is among the most effective of those functioning in America. We readily accept speaking engagements at conferences and churches. We beseech you to intercede for us as we evangelize Muslims. Our vision is global and should you be interested in learning more about our work you are invited to contact us at the addresses provided below. As we stand united in faith in Jesus, thousands of individual Muslims will testify about how they too have become a *Miracle of Miracles.*

The End

Touch of Christ Ministries

P. O. Box 2861
Fairfax, Virginia 22031
Minanevisa@aol.com
www.touchofchrist.net

For other books by Jim Croft go to www.booklocker.com and type in Croft or e-mail jcroft8942@adelphia.net. His free newsletter featuring various topics of interest to contemporary Christians may be obtained by going to www.pccchurch.org /jc_ministries.htm

Addendum

INSIGHTS INTO ISLAM'S DECEPTIONS

ISLAM VS CHRISTIANITY

The word *Islam* means, *"surrender to the will of God."* It has connections with two Arabic words. One is *tasleem*, which means, *"surrender"* or *"submission."* The other is *salaam*, which by definition conveys peace with God and one's self, harmonious interpersonal relationships, and the blessings of God. My first-hand observation is that these graces are, more often than not, infrequent experiences for those living in Muslim-controlled nations. In comparison to Christianized nations, Islamic countries have disproportionate numbers of reports of human rights violations against women, children and those of other religions.

A *Muslim* is a person who presumes that surrender to the will of God is accomplished by following the religion of Muhammad. Spiritual leaders in the Muslim community are commonly referred to as Mullahs and Imams. The holy books of Muslims are called the Koran and the Hadith. The Koran serves as their bible. It is a collection of the revelations that Muhammad alleged were given to him by Allah. These revelations began in A.D. 610 and ended at his death in A.D. 632. The Hadith is a collection of Muhammad's words and deeds according to his wives, relatives, and companions. Next to the Koran, it is the most important part of Islamic Law (*the Sharia*); its teachings are just as binding.

There are five pillars to the Islamic faith among moderate Muslims, and six among the extremists. I will list all six and add the ways in which each differs from Christianity in parentheses.

• *Shahada* is their profession of faith that states, *"There is no other God but Allah, and Muhammad is the messenger of Allah."* – (Christian conversion rests solely on repentance from one's sins and the revelation and confession that Jesus is the Son of God who was raised from the dead.)

• *Salat* is praying five times daily while kneeling toward Mecca, Saudi Arabia. These prayer sessions are mandatory and actually consist of a total of 17 units of prayer each day. Two units are performed at dawn, four each at noon, late afternoon and after sunset, and the final three are uttered after dark. – (Christians are encouraged to simply worship in spirit and in truth from any position at anytime and anywhere.)

• *Sawm* is fasting during the daylight hours of the month of Ramadan. – (For Christians fasting is an optional discipline.)

• *Zakat* is almsgiving. – (Christians are encouraged to tithe and give freewill offerings. Neither of these is mandatory for salvation.)

• *Hajj* is a mandatory pilgrimage to Mecca at least once in one's lifetime. – (Christianity has no official holy city that one is obligated to visit. Trips to historical sites in Israel are an optional privilege.)

• *Jihad* is the Koranic sanction of holy war as a religious duty to spread Islam. – (Coercion is unacceptable to Christians and the Lord they serve. They propagate the Gospel by preaching Christ to those who have an interest in Christianity.)

• Islam is a harsh religion that demands absolute obedience to the Koran and the *Sharia* laws. To question these is one and the same as questioning Allah. It offers no intimacy with a loving God. All that Muslims can expect is a life of compliance to rules and regulations in the hope that they might make paradise. Not even Muhammad had the assurance that his sins were forgiven and of his eternal fate. – (Christianity is far different. The Lord invites us to come and to intimately "reason" with Him. His true sheep are those who know and hear His voice in a two-way relationship with Him. It is not a system of adherence to specific religious rules. It is the voice of the Holy Spirit that dictates what we can and cannot do. It is about cultivating harmonious relationships with others through the grace that our right relationship with God, through faith in Jesus, provides for us. Anyone who puts his faith in Jesus has the assurance of forgiveness and eternal life)

MUHAMMAD, THE DECEIVED DECEIVER

Anyone who is familiar with the Bible, and reads either the Koran or the Hadith, can discern that Muhammad was familiar with Judaism and Christianity, and that he borrowed generously from their writings. Muhammad made the self-aggrandizing claim that he was God's (Allah's) final messenger with divine insights and an anointing that eclipsed those of his predecessors; Abraham, Moses, the New Testament's Apostles and Jesus. According to the Christian Bible, Muhammad can be identified as a deceived deceiver who was operating under the influence of a spirit of antichrist. The prefix *anti* of the word *antichrist* can mean *in place of* as well as *against.* The word *Christ* is defined as *the anointed one of God.* Therefore, a reasonable expanded definition of the word *antichrist* might read, *one who is operating in an anointing that is a substitute for the true anointing* (Heb. 1:1-3 & 1 John 4:1-3). Muhammad espoused teachings that denied the divine Son-ship of Jesus. In 1 John 2:22, it says that anyone who denies the Father and the Son is a liar of the antichrist. Muhammad also denied Jesus' death by crucifixion. He claimed that Allah told him that Jesus was elevated to heaven before His physical death. Muslims promote their Prophet's postdated revelations as superior to those of Jesus and His Apostles.

When Jesus was tempted by the devil in the wilderness, He refused to heed his voice and bow down to him (Matt. 4:1-11). Satan was successful in getting the founder of Islam to accommodate idolaters and to comply with his temptations.

Muhammad used every maneuver at his disposal to convince the polytheistic people of Mecca to embrace Islam. They worshipped 365 gods, of whom Allah was considered the ruling deity.

To appease and appeal to the pagan Arabs, Muhammad incorporated some of their idolatrous rituals into Islam. The Islamic practices of making Hajj, circling the Kaaba, and kissing the black stone are all pagan rituals that predate Islam. During one of his meetings with the chiefs of the Quraish tribe of Mecca, Muhammad took a step that exposes the depth of his deceptive desperation. He feigned devotion to their pagan deities.

He recited the following Koranic verses wherein supposedly Allah praised the three pagan Arabian goddesses, *Allat, Al-Uzza,* and *Manat.* The verses read, *"Have you not seen Allat, and Al-Uzza, and Manat, the other, the third? These are the exalted Swans, and truly their intercession may be hoped for."* Muhammad then led the Quraishites in paying homage to the goddesses by kneeling in prayer with them. Curiously, soon afterward Muhammad apparently recognized that his actions had been inconsistent with the monotheistic nature of the Islamic religion that he was attempting to establish. His remedy was to allege that Satan had whispered the verses in his ears. He nullified the verses and changed the text of Koran, Surah 53:19-23 to read as it does today.

MUHAMMAD'S EGOTISTICAL CLAIMS

Prior to my conversion, and unbeknownst to me, the Holy Spirit was leading me to question numerous things about Muhammad. I doubted that he had truly encountered the true God when he got his revelations. I also questioned his claims to be a prophet and God's final apostle. After becoming a Christian I discovered that my doubts were well founded. In this section I will cover aspects of his character that defy the premise that he was a prophet and an apostle.

Muhammad was orphaned at the age of six and was left in

the care of his grandfather, Abdel Muttalib, who was a chief in Mecca's Quraish tribe, and the keeper of the aforementioned idolatrous shrine of Kaaba. Two years later Muhammad's grandfather died and the child was passed into the care of his uncle, Abu Talib. A rich widow named Khadija, who owned a caravan trade business, employed Muhammad when he was 25 years old. Though she was 15 years senior to him in age, he eventually married her and gained the appearance of a respectable merchant. At forty years of age he became disenchanted with polytheism and began to spend time meditating alone in a cave near Mecca. That was when he supposedly received a visitation that led him to believe that he was commissioned by Allah to initiate the true religion. According to the Bible, the whole matter was a Satanic deception.

• A spiritual entity representing himself to be the Holy Spirit, as well as the angel Gabriel, gave Muhammad the "true religion" that was to replace Judaism and Christianity. According to the Bible, the Holy Spirit is a member of the Godhead, and angels are merely God-created spiritual beings. *"Say the Holy Spirit (the Angel Gabriel) has brought the revelation (the Koran) from thy Lord in Truth."* (Koran, Surah 16:102)

• There is strong evidence that the Islamic Allah is not identical to the God of the Bible. What then was he? The apostle Paul warned Christians that Satan could transform into an angel of light. He also said that he was concerned about those that would come preaching under the inspiration of a spirit that was *different* from the Holy Spirit, that would declare a *different* Gospel, that would feature *another* Christ (anointed one of God). Paul's concern was that many would be deceived into departing from authentic faith in Christ by listening to the doctrines of demons that were based on lies (2 Cor. 11:1-4, 14 & 1 Tim 4:1-2). All of this describes the events that spawned Islam.

An angel of light ("light" is a synonym for "revelation") came to Muhammad and said that he was both Gabriel and the Holy Spirit. This mixture definitely makes this being of an entirely *dif-*

ferent spiritual species than the divine, eternal Holy Spirit of God. Muhammad was deceived into believing that he was superior in anointing to Christ. This would infer *another* Christ or anointed one. The Prophet then began to proclaim the demonic doctrinal lie that he had a religion that was "better news" for mankind than the Gospel of Jesus. (The word Gospel means "good news.") So he was surely preaching a *different* Gospel. Therefore, the spiritual entity that gave revelations to Muhammad was at best a lying, deceiving spirit, and at worst Satan, the father of lies, representing himself to be an angel of light.

•   Contemporary Christians, like those of the first century church, are responsible to examine the claims of those who claim apostleship (Rev. 2:2). The biblical signs of a true apostle are perseverance and miracles (2 Cor. 12:12). Anyone who does not have ample evidence of these two graces is lying about being an apostle. Jesus and His apostles performed many miraculous cures (Act 10:38, Acts 3:1-8, Rom. 15:18-19). There are no historical accounts of Muhammad and the subsequent leaders of Islam performing miracles.

•   The absence of miracles made it difficult for Muhammad to convince people that his new religion was valid. During his first year of ministry in Mecca, only three people converted. It was his wife, his cousin and his slave. Over the first five years he had less than thirty converts. Much to his embarrassment, his uncle and benefactor, Abu Talib, was never persuaded to come into the fold. In disgusted frustration Muhammad moved his headquarters to Medina and initiated a new tactic to win converts: violence.

•   Jesus was non-violent, and He forbade His apostles to react with violence against agitators (Matt. 5:39). When Peter severed a soldier's ear with a sword in the garden, Jesus healed the man and commanded Peter to put away his sword (Matt. 26:51-52). Biblically, subsequent to the resurrection of Christ, not one of His apostles or those of the early church advocated violence as a means to spread the Gospel. History records that millions of Christians have been persecuted and martyred without lifting a hand to defend their lives. The Epistles emphatically state that anyone who is a brawler, is given to outbursts of anger, or retaliates with violence is disqualified from spiritual leadership (1 Tim. 3:3, Titus 1:7). Muhammad was a warrior who took lives to spread his message. Through the centuries, and to this day, thousands of Islam's clerics have incited violence for the cause of Jihad.

JIHAD

The Muslim worldview divides humanity into two opposing halves. One side *Dar es Salaam*, is *The House of Peace*. It is the zone where Islam rules. The other side is *Dar el Harb, The House of War*. It is the war zone that is occupied by non-Muslims. Their worldview dictates that war will continue between these two sections of humanity until the supremacy of Islam is fully established throughout the world. The history of Islam exemplifies that their preferred method of transforming nations from the *House of War* to the *House of Peace* is through *Jihad* or *holy war*. Once a nation is conquered, religious persecution and discrimination are utilized to wear down the population until everyone submits to Islam.

Jihad, holy war, was the primary vehicle that was used to spread the Muslim faith through the ancient world. From A.D. 632 through A.D. 1514 Islamic armies raped and pillaged their way from Medina, Saudi Arabia, to Iran and then onto the borders of German- and French-speaking Europe. The nations pictured in our Bible maps, that were the cradle of the Christian faith, have few Gospel-proclaiming churches left. Mosques have replaced the churches. These countries include Israel, Jordan, Syria and Turkey. The nations of North Africa, stretching from Egypt westward through Libya and Algeria and on to Morocco, were once bastions of Christianity. They all fell under the crescent moon of Islam by the 10th century.

The present-day descendants of the early Christians, unlike their forefathers, are not faith-filled believers of the Lord Jesus Christ. They are languishing as Muslims in the grip of the anti-Christ spirit of Islam. Most of the conquered were given the choice of conversion or the sword. Conversion then and now is accomplished by repeating the *Shahada* three times, *"There is no God but Allah, and Muhammad is the prophet of Allah."* During this period Christians, Jews, and other minorities that did not convert and managed to elude the sword became second-class citizens. Muslims called them *Ahl-al-Dhimma* or *Dhimmis.* This Dhimmitude status was, and remains to this day, synonymous with discrimination. They had to pay a special tax, wear distinct clothing and were denied the right to have a voice in politics.

Muslim activists cunningly attempt to defuse any notion that *Jihad's* basic definition is *holy war.* They explain the word's primary definition is *to struggle with one's sinful inclinations to rebel against the will of Allah.* They insist that Jihad is only used as a synonym for holy war in the context of defense and never as a term for hostile actions as a means of offense.

The words of Muhammad, the facts of history and the protests of Muslims in non-Western nations belie their heady assertions that Jihad is simply a benign spiritual term. The rioting crowds of Muslims that chant "Jihad" over and over indicate that the word has undergone an idiomatic transformation in their understanding. Even if its original, antiquated meaning was *"struggle,"* it is an idiom today that primarily means *"holy war that endorses terrorism."*

The reality is that over the centuries, and to this present-day, there have been no changes in Islam's goal to conquer the world. The following verses taken from the Koran and the *Al Bukhari* version of the Hadith demonstrate the undeniable truth that contemporary followers of Muhammad can find support for terrorism and Jihad through his words.

- *"Strike terror (into the hearts of) the enemies of Allah and your enemies."* - Koran, Surah 8:60
- *"Fight (kill) them (non-Muslims), and Allah will punish (torment) them by your hands, cover them with shame."* - Koran, Surah 9:14

- *"I will instill terror into the hearts of the unbelievers, smite ye above their necks and smite all their finger-tips off them. It is not ye who slew them; it was Allah."* - Koran, Surah 8:12

- Muhammad once was asked: *"What is the best deed for the Muslim next to believing in Allah and His Apostle?"* His answer was: *"To participate in Jihad in Allah's cause."* - Al Bukhari, Vol. 1:25

- Muhammad was quoted as saying: *"I have been ordered to fight with the people till they say, none has the right to be worshipped but Allah."* - Al Bukhari, Vol. 4:196

- Muhammad also said, *"The person who participates in (Holy Battles) in Allah's cause and nothing compels him to do so except belief in Allah and His Apostle, will be recompensed by Allah either with a reward or booty (if he survives), or will be admitted to paradise (if he is killed)."* - Al Bukhari, Vol. 1:35,

- When the prophet of Islam started preaching his new religion in Mecca, he was conciliatory to Christians and Jews. He told them: *"We believe in what has been sent down to us and sent down to you, our God is the same as your God."* - Koran, Surah 29:45

- This attitude changed completely when he gained numerical strength after moving to Medina. Supposedly, Allah changed his mind and told Muhammad to, *"Fight those who believe not in Allah nor the last day... Nor acknowledge the religion of truth (Islam), (even if they are) of the people of the Book (Christians and Jews), until they pay the Jizya (taxes) with willing submission, and feel themselves subdued"* (Koran, Surah 9:29).

Muslim activists do not tell prospective converts and the press that the conciliatory verses that Muhammad wrote while in Mecca were later nullified by the hostile ones written in Medina. Herein lies a distinction between the Koran and the Holy Bible. Muhammad needed a device to cover his tracks in the matter that many of the Koranic verses contradict one another. He came up with the principle of *al-Nasikh wal-Mansoukh* (the Abrogator and the Abrogated). It is based upon this Koranic verse: *"Our revelations we abrogate or cause to be forgotten, we substitute (with) something better or similar. Knowest thou not that God (Allah) hath power over all things"* (Koran, Surah 2:106).

It was his ploy to cover the mystery of Allah's apparent duplicity in relation to his latter revelations contradicting his earlier ones. The early verses are those of peace and tolerance. The latter are the cruel and hostile verses that Islamics use to justify spousal abuse, gender bias, religious intolerance and terrorism.

Out of the Koran's 114 chapters, only 43 were unaffected by this doctrine. The Bible is far different. Throughout its Old Testament the authors of each of its books were inspired to pen verses that predicted the coming of Christ and the transfer from the Dispensation of Law to the Dispensation of Grace. Due to divine inspiration they were enabled to do this harmoniously even though they lived hundreds of years apart in time. The New Testament flows in flawless unity with the Old Testament. The thread of redemption through the blood of Jesus is consistent throughout the entire Bible.

• Islamic extremists use Muhammad's phrase, *lie in wait for them with every stratagem,* to justify terrorism as an orthodox tactic of Jihad. "*Fight and slay the Pagans wherever ye find them, and seize them, beleaguer them, and lie in wait for them in every stratagem (of war)."* - Koran, Surah 9:5

• The Jihad strategies of contemporary Muslim activists are very clever. They use the good will and naiveté of Western democracies as a means to gain a foothold in unsuspecting nations. The truth of this is hidden in a chilling statement that a leading Islamic spokesman made to the Archbishop of Izmir, Turkey. - "*Thanks to your democratic laws we will invade you; thanks to our religious laws we will dominate you."* They sneak their Jihad terrorists into our countries through our lenient immigration policies. Subsequently, when the malicious intentions of the extremists come to light, and we attempt to expel them, all of the supposedly moderate Muslims scream, "Constitutional foul."

When the subject of Jihad is mentioned, well-read Muslims often bring up one of the saddest periods in Christian history. It is the era in which Christendom, like much of the Muslim world of today, primarily consisted of nations that were religious-states. During this era, Christianity mistakenly adopted an Old Testament form of religious-state governments. The Emperor Constantine launched the destructive Church-State policy in A.D. 300. Subsequently, the Church-State armies of Europe defied Christ's New Testament command that His followers were not to take up weapons in an attempt to advance the influence of the Cross of Christ through holy wars.

From A.D. 1095 through A.D. 1464, the Church-State governments of Europe initiated barbarous campaigns, called Crusades, to free the Middle East from the grip of Islamic infidels. The Crusades, however, lasted less than four hundred years. During the ensuing nine hundred years Christendom has undergone a major reformation. It no longer demands Church-State governments. As a result of the Reformation, salvation has subsequently been preached through the persuasion of the Holy Spirit rather than through the use of force.

Westernized democracies that have Christianity as a prevalent religion do not call for the citizens of fellow nations to join them in holy wars against other nations. Calls to war are issued on the basis of mutual self-defense and to facilitate freedom for politically oppressed people. In isolated instances the leader of a Westernized nation might express his personal faith when his troops go to war. However, the secular compositions of genuinely free democracies prevent them from calling for war in the name of a particular religion as a matter of national policy.

These factors point to distinctive dissimilarities between Islam and Christianity. The Koran has no New Testament. Islam has never undergone a major reformation. And, the Muslims of today are still complying with Muhammad's mandate that Islam's influence is to be spread by Muslims of every nationality uniting in Jihad against those of other faiths.

MIRACLE OF MIRACLES

THE PROBLEMATIC KORAN

In recent years Islam has launched a global campaign to lure people of other faiths into its ranks. Its strategy is cunningly deceptive. In Christian nations Muslims subtly cloak Islam in the guise of being closely akin to Christianity. They boast Koranic verses that mention Jesus and His miracles while they hide the fact that they deny His divinity and His atoning crucifixion, death and physical resurrection. Their rhetoric often employs Christian terms such as salvation, justification and sanctification. The truth is these terms do not have any historical precedent in Muslim teachings.

Muhammad claimed that he was unable to read and thus asserted that his revelation of the Koran was miraculous. There are many scholars who challenge his illiteracy, as his vocation in the caravan trade business required a generous level of competency in reading and writing. It necessitated a need to read and record the transactions between his firm and those with whom it did business. In addition, it was not he who put the Koran into a single volume. This did not occur until well after his death. Various disciples, who had known him, compiled the oral tradition of his sayings, and the fragments that had been recorded, in no less than seven different versions of the Koran. Later on in time these were put into a single volume and the rest were destroyed. Interestingly, the official Arabic version is written in an antiquated, formal style of Arabic. Relatively few of the world's Muslims are able to fluently read even the verses that make sense.

The Holy Spirit did not inspire the Koran, as it contains too many confusing contradictions. In January of 1999 the *Atlantic Monthly* magazine began a three-part series on the Koran. It was written by Toby Lester and titled, "*What is the Koran?*" In the third installment an authority on Islam was quoted as saying: *"Gerd-R Puin speaks with disdain about the traditional willingness, on the part of Muslim and Western scholars, to accept the conventional understanding of the Koran. 'The Koran claims for itself that it is "mubeen," or clear.' He says, 'But if you look at it, you will notice that every fifth sentence or so simply doesn't make sense. Many Muslims — and Orientalists — will tell you otherwise, of course, but the fact is that a fifth of the Koranic text is just incomprehensible. This is what has caused the traditional anxiety regarding translation. If the Koran is not comprehensible — if it can't even be understood in Arabic — then it's not translatable. People fear that. And since the Koran claims repeatedly to be clear but obviously is not — as even speakers of Arabic will tell you — there is a contradiction. Something else must be going on.'"*

This article provides an excellent explanation for what would otherwise be an enigma to those who attempt to study various translations of the Koran. The student soon discovers that there is a significant difference in the way various translators translate the same texts. This can be confusing unless one understands several things. The fact that the Koran has large portions that are incomprehensible even in Arabic leaves much to the discretion of individual translators. Many of them desire to present Islam in a favorable light as a religion of peace.

These often modify the Koranic texts in a manner that they believe will make their faith appear less primitive, hostile and barbarous. In many instances, they have adopted a slanted freestyle method of translating certain sections of the Koran in order to defuse the appearance of contempt for Christians and Jews. Here is an example from the new French translation of the Koran in regard to the Jews. It reads, *"The people of Israel will be twice destroyed as an innocent victim, and God will reward them by elevating them to great heights."* The old translation reads just the opposite. *"The people of Israel, after sowing corruption twice on earth for the purpose of dominating other people, will push themselves up into a position of extreme power before being punished by God."*

The Holy Bible is completely different. Unlike, Muslims, Christians have allowed all to investigate and challenge the authorship and historical accuracy of the various books of the Bible. It has weathered all storms throughout history. On the other hand, there is something virulent about the nature of

Islam that incites its adherents to violence. This phenomenon is not restricted to Arab Muslims. If authority figures of Christian democracies utter even a hint of disrespect for Muhammad or the Koran, Mullahs start issuing death decrees. Violent riots ensue in every nation that has a significant Muslim population - Indonesia, Pakistan, India, Africa and the Middle East alike. One cannot help but wonder that if Muhammad's Koran is so infallible, what is it that Muslims fear?

MUHAMMAD'S MYTHS

The Koran and the Hadiths (the sayings and actions) of Muhammad, as recorded in the Sahih Al-Bukhari, contain many of the fanciful myths of the Prophet. I call them myths because they do not agree with biblical or scientific facts or ordinary common sense. In this section I will present just a few of the myths that belie the notion that Muhammad received infallible inspiration from God and that he possessed a firm grasp on reality.

• The key to health is a diet of camel's milk and camel's urine. *"The prophet ordered them to follow his camels, and drink their milk and urine, so they followed the camels and drank their milk and urine till their bodies became healthy."* - Al Bukhari, Vol. 7:590

• You do not need to be concerned if a fly falls into your food. Antibiotics on one of its wings will neutralize any germs that might be on its other wing. *"If a housefly falls in the drink of any one of you, he should dip it (in the drink), for one of its wings has a disease and the other has the cure for the disease."* - Al Bukhari, Vol. 4:537

• Alexander the Great found the sun sitting in a pool of water while on one of his treks on the battlefield. *"They ask thee concerning Zul-qarnain (Alexander the Great) Say, 'I will rehearse to you something of his story. Verily we established his power on earth, and we gave him the ways and the means to all ends. One (such) way he followed, until, when he reached the setting of the sun, he found it set in a spring of murky water: Near it he found a*

People: We said: O Zul-qarnain! (thou hast authority,) either to punish them, or to treat them with kindness.'" - Koran, Surah 18:83-88

- The stars are missiles that God uses to knock demons from the sky. *"The creation of these stars is for three purposes; as decoration of the sky, as missiles to hit the devils, and as signs to guide travelers."* - Al Bukhari, Vol. 4 page 282

- If a Muslim fails to awaken in time for the dawn call to prayer, it is because Satan urinated into his ears. *"Narrated Abdullah: the prophet was told that a person had kept on sleeping till morning and had not got up for the prayer. The prophet said, 'Satan urinated in his ears.'"* - Al Bukhari, Vol. 2:245

RELIGIOUS INTOLERANCE

Throughout this book I have explained the extent to which I have personally experienced religious intolerance at the hand of Muslims. My dear Christian friends and relatives have been imprisoned, tortured and martyred. Had my husband and I not fled Iran, we would have suffered the same fate. This type of religious persecution is inherent within Islam and its holy books and is by no means restricted to Iran. Every Islamic-controlled nation has severe penalties awaiting any Muslim who attempts to convert to another religion, and for anyone who assists them in doing so. These penalties are based upon the Koran, the Hadith and a document of religious discrimination known as *The Pact of Omar*. Omar was the second Caliph of Islam who ruled from A.D. 637 to A.D. 644. The non-Muslim citizens of the nations that were conquered through Jihad were forced to sign it.

- Muslims do not have the human right to convert to religions of their choice. If they do, they can be punished according to the *"apostasy rule,"* which states that such persons should be punished by death. Muhammad said, *"Whoever changes his religion, kill him."* - Al Bukhari, Vol. 9:57

- Those that attempt to convert a Muslim to another faith risk severe reprisals: *"The only punishments of those who wage war against Allah and His Messenger and strive to make mischief in the land is that they should be murdered, or crucified, or their hands and their feet should be cut off on opposite sides, or they should be imprisoned."* - Koran, Surah 5:33

THE PACT OF OMAR

- We shall not build new monasteries, churches, convents or monks' cells in our cities or in Muslim neighborhoods. Should any of these fall into ruins or disrepair, we shall not repair, by day or night, those in our own neighborhoods or those situated in the quarters of the Muslims.
- We shall keep our gates wide open for passersby and travelers. All Muslims that pass our way are to be given board and lodging for as many as three days.
- We shall not hide any spy from the Muslims or give them sanctuary in our churches or shelter them in our homes.
- We shall not proclaim our religion publicly nor attempt to convert anyone to it. We shall not forbid any of our kin from entering Islam if they desire to do so.
- We shall show respect toward Muslims. If they wish to sit, we shall rise from our seats.
- We shall not seek to resemble Muslims by imitating any of their garments, turbans, footwear or parting of the hair. We shall not imitate their way of speech.
- We shall not mount on saddles, gird ourselves with swords, bear any kind of arms, or conceal weapons on our bodies.
- We shall not engrave Arabic inscriptions on our seals.
- We shall not sell fermented drinks.
- We identify ourselves as non-Muslims by clipping the fronts of our heads.
- We shall always dress in the same manner wherever we go and we shall bind the *zunar*, identifying us as non-Muslims, around our waists.

- We shall not display our crosses or our books on the roads or in the markets of the Muslims. We shall use only clappers very softly in our churches. We shall not raise our voices in mourning when following our dead. We shall not shine lights on any of the roads of the Muslims or in their markets. We shall not bury our dead near the Muslims.
- We shall not take slaves who have been allotted to Muslims.
- We shall not build houses of taller elevation than the houses of Muslims.
- We accept these conditions for ourselves and for the people of our community, and in return we shall receive safe-conduct.
- If we in any way violate these regulations, for which we ourselves stand surety, we forfeit our covenant (*dhimma*) status and shall become liable to the penalties for contumacy and sedition.

It is a well-known fact that after the Israelis reclaimed Jerusalem in the Six-Day War, they were faced with an exhaustive clean-up project at the site of Herod's temple. For years the local Muslim Arabs had been using the base of the Wailing Wall as a public toilet. This defilement was nothing less than an intentional assault on the Jew's spiritual history. The Italian journalist, Oriana Fallaci, authored a book titled *Rage and Pride*. In vivid, vernacular terms she described how offended she was about immigrant Somali Muslims defiling the grounds of a cathedral in Florence, Italy. They stained the marble edifice with their urine and filled the exterior entrance to the Bishop's Baptistery with their excrement. – *This type of behavior is simply beneath the sense of common decency that most religious people possess. Even in times of war, the soldiers of Christian countries refrain from dishonoring the belief systems of others. They take great pains to preserve their enemy's houses of worship.*

GENDER BIAS AND HUMAN RIGHTS INFRACTIONS

Women have long worked to win their rights to equality in the United States. They have achieved voting rights, the privilege of higher education and are slowly being rewarded equal vocational pay. Married women cannot be forced to have sexual relations with their husbands. Divorcees are awarded alimony in most states and are guaranteed half of the assets in others. They routinely get the custody of the children when marriages are dissolved. Widowed women in America control a gigantic portion of its financial resources.

Not so under Islam. Voting and equal educational rights are rarely afforded to women. A wife is considered to be her husband's possession. She is a sex object that is to be available for her husband to "*plough as a field*" as often as he wishes (Koran 2:223). He can physically beat her if she comes across as disloyal to him (Koran 4:34). In matters of divorce, Islamic laws are cruelly biased. A man desiring a divorce may obtain it by merely saying, "I divorce you," three times in succession to his wife. If he later has second thoughts, the process of reconciliation is bizarre.

His wife must marry another man and have sexual relations with him. To expedite the process, a husband can hire a stranger to marry his wife. Subsequent to having sexual relations with the poor woman, the hireling pronounces divorce upon her. A divorcee is apt to lose custody of her children and the potential for financial support. Widows are not the first consideration when it comes to inheriting their husband's estates. Koranic law dictates that if the husband dies and leaves no children, she gets only a fourth of his wealth. His surviving parents, brothers, uncles and etc. will get the rest. If the deceased husband leaves children, the wife gets an eighth and the children get the rest. A male child inherits double the portion of a female (Koran 4:12).

Statistics indicate that Muslims perpetrate a disproportionate number of human rights infractions to that of any other single religious group. OPEC nations import disadvantaged boys, aged four to six, to be jockeys for camel races. The children are fed meagerly to keep them light in weight. Many are seriously injured, and some have been trampled to death. Sudan, Mauritania and Kuwait actively engage in slavery. It is not unusual for convicted thieves to have limbs surgically removed. Women charged with adultery are stoned to death or receive a gun shot to the temple. Enactments of these punishments have been verified by televised documentaries on Saudi Arabia, Afghanistan and Pakistan. Often they are occasions of public entertainment. Thousands of Muslims have been taped cheering as the punishments are meted out.

To diminish sexual desires, some Muslims practice female genital mutilation: circumcision of the clitoris. This invasive procedure usually ceremoniously takes place just prior to puberty. – *In compassionate societies child labor laws have been in place for more than 150 years. Slavery is an unacceptable and prosecutable offense in every Christianized nation. The ultimate goal of Western criminal codes is rehabilitation rather than mutilation. Anyone that intentionally performs a surgical procedure that diminishes quality of life is liable for suit and prison internment.*

Islam is unique in that it routinely encourages practices that would never be considered by spiritually sensitive people of other faiths. Women and children are used as human shields in battle. It is not unusual for boys as young as six years of age to be conscripted for wartime service. Adolescent boy and girls are celebrated for decisions to become homicide bombers. Muslims are known to utilize Red Crescent ambulances to transport troops and munitions. Hospitals are commonly used as command posts for combatants. Islamic regimes make a habit of killing the wounded of opposing forces and disposing of bodies without forwarding information about the fate of their victims. The various terrorist groups that operate in Israel often mutilate dead Israeli military personnel beyond recognition. - *The Geneva Convention was designed to protect non-combatants, the wounded, those surrendering, and prisoners of war. It specifies that no one under the age of fifteen can be conscripted for war. It prohibits the use of medical care facilities to camouflage aggression. In addition, each nation must follow procedures to identify the dead and wounded of opposing forces and to send information to their families. All peace-loving nations that value fairness and the dignity of the human race make every effort to comply with the spirit and intents of its regulations.*

It is very apparent that Islam does not predispose a mindset that would motivate its adherents to initiate legislation that forbids cruel and unusual punishment. When Pakistan defeated Bangladesh in 1971, Pakistani soldiers raped 250,000 girls and women. They could do so without shame due to the cultural absolutions available to them through Islam. Soldiers of Christianized nations would have been court-martialed and executed for this offense.

In late October of 2001, the MSNBC news channel aired a documentary that was part of the National Geographic Explorer series. It featured Afghanistan. The narrator showed, and explained convincing footage that men are incited to be pro-terrorism and anti-women by Islam. Again, the finger of guilt can be pointed at Muhammad and the clerics who emphasize selected portions of his sayings from the holy books. The spiritual power that spoke to him gave him some admirable instructions about the equitable manner in which women should be treated. However, the same spiritual entity inspired him with attitudes that negated almost all of the positive revelations that had been offered. These attitudes are totally inconsistent with Judeo-Christian attitudes toward women. They are by no means reminiscent of the injunctions that our loving Heavenly Father gave about marital relationships or the treatment of women when the Holy Spirit inspired the Apostles who wrote the New Testament.

• It cannot be said that the Prophet did not enjoy the company of women. To the contrary, he must have because he had at least 11 wives and an unknown number of concubines. *"Anas said, 'The prophet used to visit all his wives in an hour*

*round, during the day and night and they were eleven in number.'
I asked Anas, 'Had the prophet the strength for it?' Anas replied,
'We used to say that the prophet was given the strength of thirty
(men).'"*- Al Bukhari, Vol. 1:268

• Muhammad married a six-year-old girl. *"Narrated
Aisha that the prophet married her when she was six years old and
he consummated his marriage when she was nine years old."* - Al
Bukhari, Vol. 7:62, no. 64

• Allah accommodated Muhammad's sexual desires.
There is a Koranic verse that allowed Muhammad to postpone
sexual intimacy with any of his wives and another that revealed
that Allah allowed him to marry his adopted son's wife. One of
his wives, Aisha, responded, *"O Allah's Apostle I do not see but
that your Lord hurries in pleasing you."* - Al Bukhari, Vol. 7:48

• Muhammad said things that denigrated women and
would lead his followers to believe that women are mentally
deficient. All of these quotes are taken from the Al Bukhari.
*"After me I have not left any affliction more harmful to men than
women"* (Vol. 7:33). *"I was shown the Hell-fire and that the
majority of its dwellers are women"* (Vol. 1:28, 301; Vol. 2:161;
Vol. 7:124). *"Bad omen is in the woman, the house and the horse"*
(Vol. 7:30). Muhammad asked some women, *"Isn't the witness
of a woman equal to half that of a man?"* The women said, *"Yes."*
He responded, *"This is because of the deficiency of the woman's
mind"* (Vol. 3:826). Muhammad to women: *"I have not seen
anyone more deficient in intelligence and religion than you"* (Vol.
2:541).

Those who are equipped with the insights presented in this
section might be developing a new perspective on Islam. Most
would hardly welcome the prospects of attending forums where
Islamic fundamentalists are speaking on human rights and
equal rights for women.

MORAL PURITY

The majority of Islamic-controlled nations have policies
demanding that women wear full-body *burkas*, or at least a

head covering, while in public, regardless of whether or not they are Muslims. They rationalize that this policy is about the modesty of Muslim women, explaining that they cover their bodies to protect their honor by reserving their physical beauty solely for their husbands. However, they neglect to speak of how women, such as myself, feel once they have been liberated from wearing such items. All I had to wear was the hijab head covering. For me, and many others, it was like receiving a new lease upon my self-esteem as a woman. Women who were forced to wear full-length burkas testify that they felt like ghost figures, without individual identities when in public.

All Islamic schools of thought stipulate that a wife's daily provision of the necessities of life depends on her willingness to be available to her husband for sex (Surah 4:24). This principle paved the way for a concept called *Zawag al-Mutaa* ("*marriage for pleasure*") in Arabic. Even though polygamy is allowed for men, it legitimizes encounters with prostitutes. It is a temporary marriage that can last for as little as a few minutes, an hour, a day, a month or whatever. The men pay the women mutually agreed sums of money for the sinful pleasures that they anticipate. After the agreed period of time the marriage is automatically absolved. Muhammad sanctioned this custom during times of war when men were away from home. Omar, the second Caliph, later abolished it. However, the Shiites, and even some Sunnis, still cling to it. Obviously, it is nothing short of legitimized prostitution and is unheard of in Christian societies.

MUSLIM BROTHERHOOD MYTH

During the past 30 years, Muslims have purposely killed more Muslims than the combined number of deaths inflicted by their non-Muslim enemies. Anyone who has kept up with Middle East events understands that the concept of the brotherhood of Islam is a myth. It does not become a talking point unless one of their nations is facing non-Muslim foes.

If Israel or the Coalition against international terrorism happens to accidentally harm civilians, the Muslim world riots in protest. There have been no international Muslim protests over the numerous incidences in which Muslim terrorists purposely maimed and killed citizens of free societies. Muslim communities around the globe take it in stride when factions within Islam commit genocide against one another in Jordan, Syria, Afghanistan, Egypt, Algeria, Tunisia, Iraq and Iran.

The war between Iran and Iraq took around 1 million Muslim lives. On various occasions, Saddam Hussein butchered tens of thousands of his own countrymen. In 1970, King Hussein of Jordan got wind that the Palestinians were going to attempt to take a portion of Jordan as their homeland. In a military campaign that is now called "Black September," he sent troops into the refugee camps of Southern Jordan and Lebanon. It is estimated that as many as 4,000 Palestinians perished in the assaults. The global Muslim community did not riot in protest of this atrocity against their displaced brethren.

During the month of February of 1982, it became apparent that Islamic extremists headquartered in Hama, Syria, were mounting an effort to make Syria an Islamic-governed state. President Hafez al-Assad took decisively brutal action. He bombarded the city with artillery and then had it bulldozed into the appearance of a giant parking lot. Amnesty International estimates that from 10,000 to 25,000 civilians were slaughtered in the siege. There were no reports of the Muslims in other nations crying out that this was a grievous injustice against innocent civilians. – *After times of armed conflict nations that are built on Judeo-Christian ethics feed and clothe displaced persons. They rebuild the nations of their former enemies. It is interesting to note that when natural disasters strike Muslim countries, one rarely sees mercy missions initiated from fellow Muslim nations rushing to their aid. There are no occurrences of relief efforts coming from Islamic societies when disasters strike non-Muslim countries. Whenever and wherever disasters occur, the world can depend upon the financial resources and the relief efforts of nations that are built on Judeo-Christian values. It is apparent that Islam is as inept at fostering merciful compassion as it is in creating fruitful economic conditions within the nations it controls.*

MUSLIMS FLOURISH IN CHRISTIAN NATIONS

Westernized nations are inhabited by millions of Islamic citizens representing most every racial group. Many of them are friendly, peace-loving people who quietly live their lives as they follow their faith. When they are privileged to live in societies that have infrastructures that are built upon Judeo-Christian values, and political climates that are unencumbered by religious fanaticism, they flourish. Significant numbers of their men and women, when given equal educational and vocational opportunities, make valuable contributions to the business communities and the fields of medicine and technology within the respective Western democracies in which they reside.

Unfortunately, this is not the case within the Islamic-governed nations. These countries do not enjoy a separation of religion and state. The clergy rules and the civil authorities enforce their policies. Education is often restricted to males, and the scholastic institutions are commonly antiquated and ill-equipped. Those who promote Islam often boast of its *"golden age."* During this period, from A.D. 700 through A.D. 1200, Europe was in the Dark Ages.

The Middle East and Asian nations that had been conquered by Islamic Jihad (holy war or struggle) led the world as they continued to make advances in the disciplines of literature, science and math. There are, however, many scholars who contend that these advances were a continuation of the groundwork that had been laid by Jews, Persians and Christians prior to the arrival of the Muslims. This is supported by the reality that by the end of the 12th century, the advances ceased in the Muslim world.

In contrast, progress was restored in Christianized nations during the Renaissance and continued through the Industrial Revolution into the high-tech achievements of the current era. Islamic countries were left sitting in the sand. One would be hard pressed to cite a single original medical, industrial, or technological innovation that has come forth from an Islamic-governed nation without the undergirding of Western influence and education. During the past 500 years the Muslims in Islamic nations have not produced one contribution to science, technology or industry in a stand-alone manner. They have no Wright Brothers, Henry Fords or Dr. Jonas Salks. Students from the global community are not lined up to apprehend visas to study at the universities of Saudi Arabia and Afghanistan. The foreign embassies of Christian countries are flooded with visa applications from Muslims who are seeking opportunities to live in the fertile environments that are built on Judeo-Christian values. It would seem that if Islam really had so much to offer, we would see people from Christian nations flocking to get work and educational visas in Islamic states.

DNA IS NOT THE PROBLEM

What caused the cessation of academic progress in the nations that were conquered by Islam? Did some DNA mutation kick in that caused people's intelligence to be altered? This could not be the case because many of the same nationalities prove to be brilliant in settings that are founded on principles other than interpretations of Muhammad's teachings. The finger of guilt points toward the Muslim religion and the teachings of its clerics. The cessation of innovation was caused by the rule of Islam from A.D. 700 through A.D. 1200. It took 500 years for it to finally take hold and totally stifle the progress of the nations that were under its influence.

In short, you can tell the value of a religion by observing the plight of nations that have lived under its influence for an extended period. If a religion has merit, it will inspire creativity from those that adhere to it. South Korea was predominantly Buddhist prior to its war with Communist North Korea in 1950. Christian nations defended South Korea, and subsequently the influence of Christianity has steadily increased. Even though its economy was devastated by the war, it has risen from the ash heaps and now has a gross national product (GNP) that dwarfs those of the oil-rich Islamic-controlled nations. Christianized South Korea's GNP for 2001 was $764.8 billion, while Islamic Saudi Arabia's GNP for 2000 was $232 billion and Communist North Korea's GNP was $21.8 billion. In contrast Haiti, before its independence from France in the 18th century, had a greater gross national product than the 13 original American colonies combined. Voodoo, mixed with Catholicism, set in, and it is now the most impoverished nation in the Western Hemisphere. Many people of East Indian heritage have engineered some of the most advanced technologies in the computer sciences. Yet, Hinduism has reduced their homeland to a nation where scores of thousands starve daily as eatable cows roam the streets. In the same manner, the Muslim sheiks of the Middle East would be riding on camels, rather than in air-conditioned Mercedes, if it were not for the oil drilling technology of Christian nations. Whenever Islam is the primary focus of a government, the majority of its citizens languish in an abased existence. If those same people immigrate to a democratic society, where the pursuit of happiness is primary and their degree of religious expression is optional, they are apt to flourish.

AMERICA, THE GREAT SATAN

Islamic supporters have a repertoire of influences to blame for the lack of progress in Islamic states. America is called the "*Great Satan.*" Clerics espouse that if it were not for America's evil influence, their citizens would be flowing in freedom, prosperity and health. How soon they forget that the wealth that their leaders squander in lavish lifestyles, and the medical advances that save their citizens from epidemics, were birthed in Westernized democracies.

Others assert that regional conflicts and harsh environments are the culprits. Interestingly, there are other nations that have experienced the same and risen above the adversities. This will be exampled by a comparison of the statistics on Islam-controlled Iran, predominantly Lutheran Iceland, and Israel.

- **Iran's stats for 2000:** arable land 10%; per capita income $6,300; infant mortality rate 28.1/1000; literacy rate 79%.
- **Iceland's stats for 2000:** arable land 0%; per capita income $24,800; infant mortality rate 3.5/1000; literacy rate 100%.
- **Israel's stats for 2000:** arable land 17%; per capita income $18,900; infant mortality rate 7.5/1000; literacy rate 96%.

The statistics that have been provided thus far in this article should provoke thinking readers to ponder the possibility that there is something grossly amiss with Islam. Basic logic dictates that the faithful should be able to overcome any real or imagined Satanic obstacles, if Allah is all-powerful and Islam is indeed a superior religion. To the contrary, Muslim-controlled regimes that demand that their citizens pray five times daily, obey the Koran, follow the dictates of their imams, fast the forty days of Ramadan, and make pilgrimages to Mecca have proved impotent in bringing reasonable prosperity to the masses within their societies.

INEPTNESS IN WAR

Interestingly, it is Islamic nations, not Christian countries, that inevitably cite spiritual motivations for engaging in war. Over the past four decades television screens across the globe have been filled with such scenes. Muslims chant Jihad and boast that Allah will give them the power to annihilate various Satanic Western democracies. To date, Muhammad's Allah has proved either inept or uninterested in fulfilling such boasts. In 1967 it only took Israel six days to defeat its Koran-incited Arab neighbors. Their victory in the Yom Kippur War of 1973 was also accomplished over Muslim forces in short order. In 1991 Saddam Hussein of Iraq claimed that Allah would give him victory against the United Nations forces in what would be the "mother" of all battles. For the Iraqi army it was the "mother" of all retreats. His troops were defeated in 100 hours. During the recent War on Iraq the Coalition forces accomplished the same in 23 days. It is notable that when Islamics go to war with one another each claims that Allah will give them the victory. If the opposing armies have actually received spiritual assurances of victory, it infers the influences of a double-minded entity whose character is inconsistent with the Living God. Muhammad's Allah and his Koran are misrepresentations of anything resembling the nature and intentions of the Divine Creator.

VALLEY OF DECISION

If you are a Muslim, I know that the contents of this addendum have been painful and perhaps infuriating. You know that the behaviors that have been cited are not rare occurrences. If you are residing in a Western democracy, you likely emigrated to escape the stifling influences endemic with Islamic regimes. I entreat you not to dismiss that which has been stated by rationalizing that every religion undergoes periods of unbecoming policies. Most religions have modified their former abusive excesses. This was done to keep pace with universally accepted standards that demand respect for every individual's right to freedom of choice. Any spiritual discipline that habitually insults basic human dignities is at risk of falling into disfavor and becoming obsolete. The seeds one sows tend to reap multiplied crops of that which was sown. If we have been intolerant of others, vast numbers will be harsher with us.

Islam's current reputation is deplorable to the global community. At this juncture, liberal France is concerned with the growth of Islamic fundamentalism. It has recently enacted a law forbidding female Muslims to wear head coverings in public institutions. Belgium is considering the same, and many provinces in Germany already have them in place. France's interior minister, Nicolas Sarkozy, is threatening to expel any foreign Muslim religious leader who disseminates extremist propaganda. Should this occur, it could eventually escalate to include every foreign Muslim. Historically, it has happened to other groups, and history does repeat itself. If France provides a precedent, other democracies could follow suit. Many want to be rid of elements that have proved to be subversive. Without question, the propensity of Islam to assert its will on non-Muslim populations is becoming increasingly disconcerting within numerous countries.

Apparently Islam's reputation is also disconcerting to those within its own ranks. Its ineptness at producing productive economies for the nations it controls and its various barbarous policies are costly. According to an article posted in 2004 on the Arabic version of the Al-Jazeera news network's website, it is losing millions of members each year. In Africa alone it is losing 6 million adherents per year. The article's complaint was that the majority of them are converting to Christianity. It also inferred serious concerns about the masses of the world's Muslim intellectuals who are making an exodus from Islam. In this regard, Iran and Western democracies have been especially hard hit. Interestingly, the reasons for departure that the educated cite are precisely the issues that I have addressed in this addendum. Surely, there is a message in all of this for you.

Muslim friend, this book has confronted you with a choice. It pertains to your earthly and eternal destiny. You are likely Islamic by birth rather than choice. Liberate yourself and your descendants by committing yourself to a religion that bears evidence of the blessings of God. Christians are not perfect, and Christendom certainly has a few problems. But, between Islam and Christianity, when it comes to objective evidence of God's affirmation, Islam is overwhelmingly outweighed. As you ponder these matters, there are questions that you must resolve. What is it about Islam that causes its adherents to engage in, or to routinely acquiesce to, practices that other religions find objectionable? Does the content of the Koran have a greater tendency to enhance people's compassion for their fellow man or their inclination for barbarism? Is there any objective evidence that God endorses Islam more than any other religion? If you had not been born into a Muslim family, would the overall quality of life demonstrated by the world's Muslim populations attract you to Islam?

INVITATION TO EXPERIMENT

Hopefully, you are willing to engage in an experiment that has transformed the lives of thousands of Muslims. As you have seen from reading this book, God has a special love for Muslims. He often reveals Himself to those of us from Islamic backgrounds through supernatural experiences that are out of the ordinary from that which most Christians experience. My husband, father, and I all received supernatural dreams and visions in which the Lord revealed Himself to us and pointed us to the way of salvation through Jesus Christ. We heard His voice speaking our names. God the Father knows your name. Jesus is waiting for your heart cry to know the True and Living God. His desire is that you no longer labor to appease a remote god who gives you no assurances that your prayers are heard.

Here is the experiment with which I challenge you: Ask God the Father to reveal Jesus to you through the power of the Holy Spirit. I assure you that you will not be disappointed. He has appeared to thousands of Muslims in various ways. He will grace you with a spiritual encounter that will thoroughly convince you that Jesus is the Living Son of God. He knows that the spiritual obstacles that Islam has established in your heart require extraordinary signs to convince you that Jesus is the Way. Therefore, He routinely gives Muslims supernatural revelations like the one that my father experienced.

Such are the vehicles that He uses to launch Muslims, like you, into lives of joyful, intimate, two-way relationships with Himself and His Son, Jesus. You have nothing to lose and everything to gain by saying that simple prayer. It revolutionized our lives. Yours can be too. It is something wonderful, why shouldn't you experience it? It is my prayer and life calling that you and your family will be freed from the deceptions of Islam.

ESPECIALLY FOR MUSLIMS

Unless a minister was either born into a Muslim home or has studied Islam for years, they have no conception of the challenges that Muslim converts to Christ face. Few understand the peer pressures and the intensities of the spiritual warfare that can assault you. I was born to a Muslim family and was thoroughly indoctrinated in Islam from infancy. I want to share some insights with you that will make your journey as a new Christian easier than that which I initially experienced.

• **Know your enemy** – You have previously been a devotee to a religion that is empowered by the Satanic spirit of anti-Christ. Satan will use every device and every demon available to disrupt your enthusiasm for your newfound faith. For this reason you must avail yourself of every spiritual weapon in God's vast arsenal. You will need to sleep, eat, and drink the Word of God. Every time the devil pops a negative thought about Christianity into your mind, you must respond instantly with praises and confessions of what the Bible says the blood of Jesus has done on your behalf. Along with that, you should command the spirits of unbelief and discouragement to leave you in Jesus' name. This is what the Bible defines as resisting the devil. Its promise is that he will flee from you.

• **Repent and renounce** – Your years of quoting the Koran and reciting the *Salat* have established a stronghold in your heart and mind that must be broken. Repent of your homage to the Koran and ask the Lord to shatter its walls in your mind. It is also helpful to sever the soul-tie that you might have to the Mullah whose voice you followed as he taught you Koranic verses in Arabic. That can be accomplished by specifically renouncing him by name. And last, but not least, it is essential that you renounce Muhammad's Allah and the *Shahada*.

• **Confess through Jesus' blood** – The following is a prayer that will liberate you from all of the aforementioned bondages. *Through the blood of Jesus, all of my sins are forgiven. I am redeemed, cleansed and forgiven by the blood of Jesus. I hereby* *repent of every connection that I have had with Islam. I renounce the concepts that Muhammad's Allah is God and that the Shahada is a godly confession of faith. I do not believe that Muhammad was a true prophet and apostle. God is One by the fact that three distinct divine persons, the Father, the Son and the Holy Spirit, flow in unified harmony.*

I believe that Jesus Christ of Nazareth was physically raised from the dead by the Holy Spirit. Jesus is my Prophet who gives direction to my life. He is the Apostle of my faith who empowers me to overcome Satan. The Koran is not divinely inspired, only the Bible is the true Word of God. I renounce the Mullah (insert his name) who taught me the Koran. I sever the umbilical cord of any soul-tie to him in the name of Jesus. The Word of the Lord is like a hammer that breaks the rocks in pieces. It now shatters the demonic Koranic and Sharia walls of Islam in my heart and mind.

From this point forward Satan and the anti-Christ spirit of Islam have no power over me, and no unsettled claims against me. Islam and Satan are vanquished from my life by the blood of Jesus. My body is the temple of the Holy Spirit. The members of my body are instruments of righteousness, yielded to God for His glory and His service. I will never again kneel toward Mecca. I will worship the Living God in spirit and truth anywhere, at anytime. Lord, I praise Your name that I am a new creation in Christ Jesus. For me, all things are new and all things pertaining to me are of God. In Jesus' name, amen!

- **Experience baptisms** – The foundation doctrines of the Christian faith are found in Hebrews 6:1-3. They are repentance from dead works (adherence to the *Sharia* in an effort to appease Allah is a work that produces death); faith toward God; the doctrines of baptisms; laying on of hands; the resurrection from the dead; and the eternal judgment. Your building permit to advance in Christian maturity is predicated upon becoming familiar with these doctrines. Notice the use of the plural form of the word for *baptism*. There are two types that are essential for you. One is baptism in water by immersion. The other is the baptism in the Holy Spirit. **Baptism in**

water is not an empty ritual like Islam's ablutions, which have to be conducted five times daily before performing each session of the *Salat*. It is a onetime initiation into Christianity that is your personal identification with the death, burial and resurrection of the Lord Jesus Christ. When you are immersed you are demonstrating that when Jesus died and was buried that by faith you were in Him and were also simultaneously buried.

The Muslim who once feared breaking one of the *Sharia Laws* is dead and buried. As you arise from the waters of baptism you are signaling that when Jesus arose from the dead, you also arose from the dead. You are no longer the slave of Muhammad, but rather a member of the Body of Christ and a beloved child of God. I heartedly suggest that you do the following when you are baptized in water. Tell the minister what your chronic problems are with sin, emotional issues and your health. Ask him to state that those specific problems are being buried as he puts you under the water. Then ask him to proclaim that as you come forth from the waters that you are arising to newness of life. Through the years many people have testified that this practice has liberated them from lifelong troublesome issues. **The baptism of the Holy Spirit** is an immersion in the Holy Spirit that comes at your request, subsequent to your salvation experience. It equips you with the supernatural gifts of the Spirit that will enable you to function in power, as did the early apostles.

• **Get into a good fellowship** – Regular sessions of fellowship are the lifeblood for all believers. While you listen to sermons it edifies your spirit. The other members of the church have gifts of the Holy Spirit that you need exercised on your behalf. Likewise, you have gifts that they need. God has designed the Body of Christ in a manner that partially makes us interdependent upon one another on the earthly plain, as everyone looks to the Lord and is filled with the Holy Spirit.

• **Stay in the Word and prayer** – Reading the Bible in a language that you understand is not like it was when you read the Koran in Arabic and attempted to decipher meaning from its confusion. The author of the Bible is the Holy Spirit. Each time that you prayerfully approach His Word He is there, as your onsite personal guide. You will hear the voice of God and receive guidance for every aspect of your life, as you read the Bible. The power of prayer cannot be overemphasized. It is your most viable tool in warding off the powers of evil and apprehending God's best for you and your family. It should always be punctuated by intermittent praise and thanksgiving to God.

• **Witness** – Share your testimonies of God's power in your life with everyone who will listen to you. Be bold enough to step out in faith by praying for people's healings. Those who have been healed of sicknesses as the result of your prayers are much more apt to listen to the Gospel through you.

By personal experience, I can promise that if you follow these steps, you will enjoy a victorious Christian life. That is my prayer for you. Please contact Touch of Christ Ministries if you have any questions pertaining to the Spirit-filled life in Christ. We also eagerly await the testimonies of what God has done in your life.

Visit: **www.touchofchrist.net**

or write to:

Mina Nevisa
P.O. Box 2861
Fairfax, VA 22031